TECHNICAL CHANGES WITH HUMAN RESOURCES

TECHNICAL CHANGES WITH HUMAN RESOURCES

By

Dr. Shoeb Ahmad

Associate Professor

Deptt. of Management

Bahir Dar University

Ethiopia

DISCOVERY PUBLISHING HOUSE PVT. LTD.

NEW DELHI-110 002

Published by:
Tilak Wasan
DISCOVERY PUBLISHING HOUSE PVT. LTD.
4831/24, Ansari Road, Prahlad Street
Darya Ganj, New Delhi-110002 (India)
Phone: +91-11-23279245, 43764432
Fax: +91-11-23253475
E-mail: parul.wasan@gmail.com
discoverypublishinghouse@gmail.com
info@discoverypublishinggroup.com
web: www.discoverypublishinggroup.com

First Edition: **2011**
ISBN: 978-81-8356-829-6

Technical Changes with Human Resources

Printed at:
Shree Balaji Art Press
Delhi

Dedicated
To
My Parents

Preface

This book is written with the actual or aspiring human resource manager in mind, but should also be of value to the general manager and administrator. It should apply equally to those in the private, public and not-for-profit sectors of the economy. Because, it considers a number of techniques and perspectives that can be employed by the organisation in order to meet that challenge.

It will be specifically appropriate for the students for whom human resources management forms a specific part of their study. Besides, to prepare executives to solve complex human problems effectively and making optimal use of human resources in organisational settings.

The book consists of 13 chapters dealing with technical change with human Resources – manpower management in 21st century, manpower planning, role of technology in human behaviour, recruitment and selection, training and development, emerging trend in human resources, etc. The basic aim is to provide information on manpower development covering particularly manpower in an integrated approach to the study of the management aspect depending on the specific physical and economic characteristics.

I have presented a detailed study of the contribution of technological changes in economic growth, increased productivity, etc. I have aptly analysed the role played by technological advancement in social alterations, economic influence and political pressures.

In addition, the technological changes under constraints of manpower follow different patterns to accomplish the social goals. In retrospect, there is no single model of modernised technology, but rather a cluster of concepts that deals with modernisation across many sectors of national economies. Significant questions have been added at the end of each chapter. Moreover, useful cases have been included to help the reader strengthen and broaden his understanding of the subject. It is intended to be not only a set of readings but an organic whole providing a coordinated, concise and integrated treatment of the subject.

I am indebted to everyone in my circle of educationists for getting inspiration to write a book in the area of 'Manpower development'. It's my great pleasure to express my heartful gratitude to my beloved parents and wife who have shouldered by burdens for the successful completion of my book.

I am thankful to my publisher Discovery Publishing House, New Delhi for publishing the book timely. Suggestions from the reader are most welcome to make the book useful for the students.

DR. SHOEB AHMAD

Contents

Cases

Sierra Textiles Limited

Sierra Textiles Limited has witnessed upheavals in its business journey. It was initiated by Mr. Arora in the year 1986 with its plant in Kolkata. Today its brags of 4 plants in Kolkata alone. It has a whopping turnover being in the vicinity of 600 crores. It has technical expertise from a Korean giant and it is the supplier of jeans the company has been facing vagaries but it has retained its position as one of the leading companies in the textile sector. The company has the mix of young and experienced operative manpower the old and new technology is manning this textiles industry.

Mr. Bipul Mehra, son of the founder of the textiles industry is concerned at the colossal investment on the latest technology automation computerisation and recruitment of qulified manpower. The training of workers, supervisors and managerial manpower has been carried out by fits and starts.

Mr. Vijay heads the eastern region. The upgradation of technical skills was the dire need of the company. He opines that new technology made it necessity the immediate skill upgradation of the old workers and educating new entrants.

Mr. Sinha who heads the Western Regional Head points out that the customers especially the foreign buyers and demanding product quality. Mr. Ashok, the head of the personnel department is exposing manpower to quality improvement programmes.

Mr. Sinha who heads the Southern Region is emphatic on training policy and skilled personnel.

Mr. Mehra opines—I am of the opinion that a company like our should groom men with its own premises away from the workplace.

Mr. Bhandari is of the opinion that I am open to the idea of satisfying the direct need of training in the company.

1. Develop a model of a training system in the company.
2. Do you feel a training institute would help in meeting. The training needs of Sierra Textiles Ltd. Give reasons.
3. Which type of research work can be successfully earned out in am institute attached to a corporate entity as the one encouraged by Bipul Mehra?

Allahabad Bank

The Allahabad Bank was incorporated in 1958 with its Head Office at Mumbai. It has mushroomed all over India. It is one of the well-staffed banks in the country. The Bank has set up regional offices in metropolis. The strength of its employees has shot up immensely with the nationalisation of Banks. This Banks has re-oriented its polices. Crash programmes have been introduced. This Bank has been allotted many districts in Punjab, Bihar, Chennai, Madhya Pradesh, Uttar Pradesh. This Bank is giving a lead to other banks in states. Each branch is doing a commendable job in giving loans to poor farmers. It is financing the people to better their miserable lot. In the agricultural field its job is remarkable indeed. The businessman have profited from this bank.

The comprehensive Corporate Reorganisation plan has been introduced to cope with problems stemming from the growth and diversification process. The reorganisation ushered a change in duties at various levels. There is a functional division at the Head Office and regional offices the area and Branch offices handled all aspects. A large number of technical officers such as engineers and agricultural officers, accountants and managers have been recruited to look after manpower planning recruitment training and evaluations.

The Bank achieves rural penetration and it is eradicating regional imbalances. This Bank is growing and spreading its tentacles in the remote areas. The managers are trying to hike deposits in their Banks.

The Staffing, Evaluation and Career Efflorescence

The total staff has gone up from lakhs to crores. The hierarchical levels range from Grade E to Grade A special in the officer category.

The Bank has dispersed geographically in large states and districts with many employees.

The Method of Training in Bank

The training function was impressive indeed. Since a large number of persons have been required their training activities must be stepped up to give excellent and prompt services to customers.

The clerical and subordinate staffs were manning the different branches. The Bank had to bank on the job training. There was a stupendous spurt in expansion activity. It was trying to relieve a good employee for attending training courses unwanted staff got sent for training event it resulted in waste of time.

Mr. Kumar took over the charge of manpower development. The faculty work was deviation from the normal career path and hence it was difficult to get competent people with a flair for teaching.

Requirement for perspective plan for training

Mr. Praashad was preparing a pins perspective plan for training and he supported for training required officers at various level.

Questions

1. What are the training need of Allahabad Bank?

2. What are the obstacles faced by Mr. Kumar and why?
3. Prepare a blue print of recommendation for training in Allahabad Bank.

Crisis in Industries

The Sona Limited is a colossal public sector company which produces fertiliser. This company has established the fertiliser unit in the remote backward rural areas as per government directives. The company keeps in mind the uplift of the poor masses of the area. Hence it has recruited semi-skilled and unskilled employees from the villages and town. The local workers constitute the major chunk in the company.

The company has sophisticated technology in the output of fertilisers. The company follows the policy to hire engineers from recognised institutions as management trainees and to train them for junior management cadre. The junior management of the unit comprises around 100 young engineers. The company has residential colong for employees near the factory.

At the outset the relations between the junior managers and workers were not cordial. The indiscipline on the part of workers industrial problems. This stand of the senior managers threw cold water on the enthusiasm of junior engineers. They began to look for jobs elsewhere. In the past the turnover of young experienced engineers was high which gave anxious moments to the management. The performance of the company was not satisfactory as the production of fertilisers was obstructed, thanks to technical limitations.

When the situation took a worse turn, the untoward incident occurred in the bagging plant. A junior technical engineer Mr. Bose was entrusted with the task of repairing and maintaining a bagging machine to be finished within a weak by the plant manager who chafed under onerous pressure, thanks to technical problems of his area. Three days after the assignment of the job. Mr. Bose found the progress satisfactory behind plans and it was owing to the casual stance of workers under his baton. On the fourth day he called all his employees on the shop floor and explained the unsatisfactory progress of the job. He also went on to explain the cause of delay, uttering how it was a sine-qua-non in the interest of the company and all workers ought to keep their heads down and to finish their assigned tasks in time.

One of the workers, Mr. Saha, the Union leader put forth issues like production incentives overtime, canteen services, quality etc. which were not properly attended to by the management. If the company turns Nelson's eye to the demands of workers the workers should not bother about the company's interest.

Mr. Bose reported that these things should be looked into by the Junior-managers and the workers could not invent excuse for delaying a job. Mr. Bose's remark had no impact and the workers under him began with their casual approach with the backing of Mr. Saha. While reporting facts to the Plant Manager Mr. Saha was given a letter of warning after reading, which he started hurling invectives at Mr. Bose threatening him with the direct consequences. This was noticed by Junior Engineers in the plant and workers on shop-floor. Being enraged Mr. Bose reported the incident to the Plant Manager who gave him assurance to look into the matter.

All Junior Engineers thronged in the colony and decided to cease work. Mr. Saha was sacked. All Junior Engineers gathered at the factory gate and informed the G.M. of their decision. The HR Manager explained that no worker be sacked without an enquiry the GM asked the HR Manager for issuance of suspension orders. Mr. Saha was put under suspension pending the enquiry.

The union representatives met the GM demanding withdrawal of suspension orders failing which they threatened to go on strike. The GM urgently convened a meeting of Senior Managers to pursue the matter. The majority was of the opinion that strike at this stage would administer severe setback to the company which is plagued by crisis and the top priority should be given to continue production and this warding off strike, they were of the opinion that Junior Engineers could be persuaded to resume their duties by giving assurance of non-recurrence of such an untoward incident.

What are the pros and cons of new technology in an industry?

Answer the following questions

The General Manager obliged the majority and withdrew the suspension order issued to Mr. Saha.

Was the decision taken by the GM justified?

What will be the result of the GM's decision?

What decision would you have taken as GM?

Technological Grooming INC

Technological Grooming Inc. has been sponsored to generate and distribute videotaped courses lectures. The market research experience and confabulations with Mr. John president of the company that the demand for his product would not justify operations. A buries of lectures for one course had been engendered, but sales of it were disconcerting. Students who watched the Tapes chorused that they preferred a live teacher even though they were not savvy as the video lectures.

Mr. John had in vested $ 30,000 from his funds and had spent a year as full timer for the company. He concluded that he would dismantle the company, he could not recover his $ 30,000 and he took decision that further investments would be quite unfair.

1. Two conditions are must in biological and social system for innovations—new species organism or organisation that survives.

First a mutation (novel system) seconds an ambience buttressing the mutation. Catalogues the disaster of the company in ecological biological analogs terms.

2. Delineate the resources technological grooming Inc. has taken from its environment and how its outputs are prized by the environment where did this interaction collapse, triggering the failure of the company.
3. What steps might Mr. John take to make his ambience more supportive of his organisation? Do you think he could be crowned with success? Why?

Computer Revolution

Mr. Bright heads the accounting section in a fast growing manufacturing company. In the section the 50 employees under his control. The company has five hundred employees who are from nearby areas. The tremendous changes in Science and Technology have spurred management to introduce mechanisation in the accounting section. Mr. Bright is asked to explicate the import of having to his employees. The introduction will have to restructure their job responsibilities, ten employees need grooming in the handling of computer and the remaining ten may have to knock at the doors of other companies for jobs.

The scenario is akin to another situation visualised by Mr. Bright some time back six months ago the company procured a computer on a lease basis to handle the production inventory. The management is pleased with the arrangement for the inventory processing has improved tremendously. But unfortunately the production propel have resisted the step vehemently. Mr. Bright is in straits. Strange enough he is given the responsibility of introducing the computer in his own section.

Questions

1. Suppose, you are head of the particular unit and you are consigned to install computer, how would you manage to inform your subordinates about the proposed change and make them favourable?

Chapter

1 Manpower Management in 21st Century

CONCEPTS

The top management in every organisation decides the role and scope of human resource functions. The essential role of human resource department is adequate use of human resources, team building and constructive employee relationships and their personal development. It is achievable by hiring skilled competent people, effective supervision, and employees motivation.

A human resource manager's method of working and attitude go a long way in deciding an organisation's performance. Social norms and cultural changes also influence an organisation's working. For example, changing labour legislations and consequent prescriptions demand a fullfledged separate department. A human resource manager has to keep himself abreast of all tribunal judgments and provide according to the changing environment. He has to be proactive and innovative that needs far sightedness besides dedication.

DIMENSIONS

Keeping in view the fast changing work environment, a human resource manager has to keep himself in close touch with all labour schemes and work for the possible implementation. Here, again all depends on the human resource manager's awareness, attitude and keenness to adopt an integrated approach keeping all dimensions—cultural, social, political and legal in view. He has to constantly study and explore new schemes that meet all these norms. Some of the new dimensions are as below:

Welfare Schemes

This needs greater involvement on the part of human resource manager to feel for the employees. He has to go beyond the labour legislations already provided and devise how the spirit of such provisions like insurance, compensations etc. can be effectively implemented to keep them motivated and attached. He has also to execute other related schemes involving education, housing, training, family welfare, retirement benefits etc.

Worker's Education

The human resource manager has to constantly upgrade worker's level of education schemes like night schools, adult education schemes and raise their literacy level. The scheme should be extended to worker's families too so that all work environment may improve.

Training Programmes

Training enhances vision and makes people multiskilled. It also betters their performance as they learn the art of doing their jobs better and with improved efficiency. It removes frustration and inspires greater involvement. The human resource manager has to proactively think and devise what sort of training should be most suitable for particular sections or personnel.

Housing and Family

The housing within reach of duty place is always helpful both to the organisation and the workers. A long commutation to work is time wasting and also affects efficiency besides shooting up functioning costs. Further, a mentally disturbed employee's outfit will be inferior compared to a happy and satisfied workers. Hence, a human resource manager should look for provisions of suitable housing and also provisions like childcare centers where working women can have their children and function with a free mind.

India being a country with diversities, a human resource manager has also to work for integration and cordiality among different groups and comparatively workers classes. Besides, legislative protection a human resource manager has to institute a working environment full of cordiality, harmony and co-operation where even physically handicapped feel confident and deliver optimum to the organisation.

Preparing Employees for Technology

People by nature resist changes as they make them learn new technology that taxes energy as well as mind. Besides, there is also general prejudice against new technology being capital intensive and anti labour. A human resource manager has a crucial role to educate and convince workers that new technology improvements are essentially for improvement in their efficiency and not for their retrenchment. Technology makes their working easier and relaxed. A human resource manager has to manage that all introduction to new technical changes are peaceful, willing and supported by staff with no apprehensions about their future welfare.

R & D Activities

An active human resource manager keeps on constantly evaluating the impact of various policies and programmes and modifies the scheme accordingly. All old and new policies have to be carefully studied and analysed and human resource manager has to come to a composite synthesis of all and formulate a new practical acceptable strategy. While doing such study a human resource manager has to calculate the usefulness and acceptability by the employees beside the level of efficiency improved, following the scheme implementation. A well researched human resource manager is fully aware of the likings and dislikings of employees as well as immediate and long-term impact of a policy over the efficiency, reputation and profitability for the organisation.

Centralised Record and Processing

In modern personalised administration, a human resource manager has to keep full relevant information about every employee available with him at just a mouse click. He has to know every potential employee intimately, his skills, suitability, capacity, temperamental proximity, willingness to learn new things as well as loyalty. While salary data is usually centralised, a human resource manager needs to maintain a centralised dosier on relevant employees and place them according to their suitability and provide for training if required to make up in the new job. Besides, centralised data have to be maintained on employees' contribution to the organisation, punctuality, absenteeism, capability, decision making ability, suitability for types of jobs, efficiency in terms of money etc.

New Concepts and Practices

A lot of new ideas, theories and practices are being deliberated and put into effect to make organisation more effective and relevant in the society. A human resource manager has to remain constantly aware of these emerging concepts and judge their relevance for their organisation.

Complete Quality Control and Management (TQM)

The concept has been enumerated by US born Demings who propounded 14 principles for maintaining and promoting top quality of goods and services, unnecessary for an organisation survival. Demings studied Japanese working closely and emphasised constant quality improvement in goods and services in order to keep customer satisfied, assured and free from after sale complaints, etc. He prescribed that organisation and management should have

- full commitment to perpetual quality improvement in products and services managed through constant critical supervision, flexibility to adopt new philosophy accelerating productivity while enhancing customers satisfaction.

- involvement of the entire organization departments in TQM as one team through improved system of production, education and training.
- absorbing new technology and methods through adequate investment, encouraging modern methods of supervision.
- infuse confidence in employee.
- free and frank discussion and exchange of views among different departments and people.
- discouraging artificial show of strength including slogans, posters etc.
- removing statistical jargons and numerical quotas.
- promoting workmanship by giving proper recognition to daily and hourly workers.
- A human resource manager has to equip himself with specific knowledge about tools and techniques.

Assessment Centres (AC)

Here are simulated real life problems that a manager is likely to face at work. The exercises involve decision making, follow-up and team working. Such exposure helps improving leadership qualities and also planning and motivation of people. Frequent exposure to such exercises also helps managers to identify strengths and weaknesses of individuals as well as the system that ultimately helps in proper planning. To make ACs system effective, organisations must have multiple assessment techniques and have simulated exercises. There should be varied assessors, pooling and sharing of informations among them for overall education of the assessees' conduct and performance. It has been found that AC judgments are accurate and predict well about future development. It's recommendations can be applied and modified according to varied types of jobs and their nature.

Quality Maintenance (QC)

This consists of a group of assessors from different departments who analyse performance and judge it's adherence to prescribed standards. They also analyse the bottlenecks if any and have brain storming sessions to research how the required standards can be maintained and further improved. They play a useful role in organisations development and progress, pay full regard to human relations and employees job satisfaction and suggest measures to workers operating to their full capability, potential and satisfaction. Principle behind QC is that people understanding their job have better performance and deliver quality results. QC members work on voluntary basis and work during company working hours and tackle the problems of their departments only. They are acknowledged for their contribution but do not get any financial compensation. A skilled seasoned and trained member from management helps to coordinate their functioning for smooth run and removing of confusion or lack of clarity, if any.

Such teams are already under operation in some organisations while many others are waiting for implementation after judging the results at others.

Conclusion

Since such measures aim at quality improvement and team work involving employees, they are being given widespread acceptance in management circles. The human resource managers have to educate the employees about such measures and extending their cooperation. In future, human resource manager's functions will embrace everything. He has to take over the responsibility and knowledge of all departments including production, finance, marketing, security, etc, besides personnel. Work environment and scope of organisation work is rapidly changing. Management and personnel have to spell their policies and objectives very clearly wherein they have to lay equal emphasis on genuine employees welfare measures besides higher and quality production. Emphasis has to be on training and development needs of the employees besides a dedicated planning for their future growth involving better facilities for their family members, too. That approach is necessary for greater involvement of employees in the development of an organisation. A human resource manager has a crucial role to play as on his initiative, dedication and tact depends the growth and success of the organisation.

MODEL QUESTIONS

1. Focus on manpower management in 21st century.
2. What are new concepts and practices?
3. What do you understand by TQM?
4. Discuss centralised record processing, assessment centres and quality maintenance.

Chapter 2

Environmental Context of Human Resource Management

An organisation is an open system which needs to interact with the environment for its continuous operation and integrating the activities of the units. So, managers must coordinate the activities of the entire organisation. In doing so, they recognise that an organisation is an element of the larger system consisting of individuals, organisations and institutions that make demand on the organisation because of their dependency and for some valued outcome. To make organisation achieve objectives and survive in the long run, the managers must manage the separate elements of the organisation itself.

There are many resources of an organisation like men, material, money and machines. But, the human resource is recognised as the most vital and valuable. Because, the success of an organisation depends upon the quality of human resources and the human resource appreciates in value as it gains more knowledge, experience and efficiency with the passage of time and use, whereas other resources depreciate in value.

Commonly there are two environments that affect organisations operation, like—

- Internal Environment
- External Environment

INTERNAL ENVIRONMENT

The major components of internal analysis are resources and competences.

Resource

Any thing, living or dead is put to use for some specific purpose/reason may be seen as a resource depending upon it's use objective and characteristics.

It can be divided into four categories like—human resource, financial resource, physical resource (buildings, stock and equipment) and intangible resource(know-how, patent, legal right, brand name, good will,...).

Human Resource: The total skills, knowledges, ideas and experiences of the human beings specific to personnel attached to an organisation is human resource and the management of the same is human resource management.

Financial Resource: These are the assets which are invested by the owner from personal deposits, borrowed from lenders collecting through selling stocks and bonds..., that is required to cover operation costs, research and development costs and expansion costs. If an organisation has got enough financial resources to do all these and other financial activities, it is financially strong and can capture any arising opportunities when this financial strength is backed by other organisational resources.

Physical Resource: It includes buildings, machines and equipments, the location of the organisation for different infrastructural services and layout of offices and plants..., these also affect the performance of the organisation. For Example—the nature of machineries and equipments (latest or outdated) affect the quality and quantity and cost of products being produced.

Intangible Resource: Which include know-how, patent, legal right, reputation and goodwill, brand name also have their own roles to play for organisations smooth, uninterrupted and successful operations. A company known for producing a particular high quality product will have better chance to be successful and get customer for new product it produces with this same brand than that of unknown company.

Competence

It is an attribute or a collection of attributes possessed by most companies in an industry. Without such attributes a business cannot survive.

In a company competence can be developed from resources, practical knowledge, skills, technology etc. The competence and core competency in other words is the strong side of the internal organisational variables that makes firms to be competent and if possible be a winner. The result of distinctive capability is an output which customer value higher than competitors. It is based on superior organisational knowledge, information, skill, structure relationship and reputation.

The internal environment reveals the organisation objectives, policies, formal structure and human resource system. The human resource system relates with organisational objectives.So, the quality of human resources must be considered while achieving the goal, because, it is the base of everything right from the objective till the achievement of a goal. In developed countries like U.S, Canada etc. the quality of human resources is more important than their designations and numbers. The goal of the people is result oriented. In context of an organisation they can do multifarious work apart from the assigned responsibilities. They don't take it otherwise. A manager doesn't need for a subordinate everywhere to assist in his work. For example, if he has to impart training on certain areas he prepares the material, do the typing, arrange the class and also handles different instrument while imparting the training likewise he can perform many works in relation to other tasks, while a person of his stature is not supposed to do that way in other branch of the same company based in our country.

We don't care for the quality. Our only objective is to achieve the position whether we deserve for that or not. In many Indian companies hierarchy is lengthened to accommodate more and more managers whether they are skilled or not. This is the reason we can't make proper objective, policies, formal structures as well as human resource systems.

EXTERNAL ENVIRONMENT

The external environmental forces are those that operate beyond a firm's boundaries and affect its operations.They include economic, demographic, socio-cultural, politico-legal and technological influences. Let us see the impact of these forces one by one.

A. Economic

From the economic point of view human resources has it's importance at national, enterprise and individual levels of analysis. According to Ginzberg, human resources are the key to economic development. But, they are being wasted through unemployment, lack of skills, lack of work opportunities, poor personal practices and the hurdles of change. These resources are responsible for a large part of output and also they have scope for enhancing productivity through their proper development.

The physical resources can't give results unless the human resources are applied to them. In addition to, if it provides value to physical resources then physical resources can provide a dynamic character to the economy. But, the human resources also have negative aspects. A poorly trained workforce may prove disastrous to the national economy. And, if the national output doesn't increase faster than it's population, the standard of living will decline. Since, it has importance at the enterprise level, so there is urgent need for the effective utilisation of human resources to attain the organisational goals. And this can be accomplished by understanding the nature, potentialities and the limitation of these resources, so develop them to their full potential, utilise them to the optimal ability of the enterprise, maintain their quality and amalgate them with other resources.

The core issue is regarding developing the economic institutions that starts with a government that develops and enforces the law to define and protect the right. Igniting growth and it's sustenation are distinct challenges that requires different sets of policies and approaches. Economic dynamism creates a fertile environment not only for the incumbents but also for the entrants and the new activities.

Business Regulations: Business are set of rules, compliance, procedures and a moral and ethical behavioural norms designed to constrain /compel the behaviour of individuals to maximise wealth or utility of principles. Business affects the process of capital accumulation as well as the process of converting this capital into output both of which are key to economic growth and poverty reduction.

The ease of doing business is very important. The cost and time to strart up and close a business are lower in China as compared to other countries in Asia-Pacific. According to World Bank report of 2004, it is harder to do business in India than China. Example of this fact is that that in 2004 it took 89 days to start a business in India but it took only 41 days to start a business in China. In addition, India also has more strict labour laws with the result it is much harder to hire and specially fire workers. This is also an impediment to growth in business. Senior management in Indian firms pay more attention towards the regulatory issues than the management of Chinese firms. The government officials in India who are responsible for overseeing the various rules and regulations have more discretion over what rules and regulation they enforce. With the result they seek higher rent than other developing countries.

Labour Market and Employment: Rigid labour market makes the firm helpless to hire and fire workers in response to shocks to technology, relative prices of outputs and inputs and the macroeconomic environment. Moreover, trade reforms needs substantial amount of intersectoral labor reallocation as well as intrasectoral labour reallocation across firms.

Another factor, that has adversely affected the efficiency of the private sector in India is the web of rules that makes restrictions at the entry and the exit of firms. Such restrictions limit the competition that are faced by existing firms and thus lower their efficiency. They also prevent the firms to exit from the market. Thus, the productivity of the industry as a whole gets affected.

Innovation: Indian firms present a full spectrum of technological capabilities. But, there are few firms at international level in terms of product design capability and process technology. Technological capabilities of most of them are inefficient, inferior quality, limited range and high costs. So, they can't face the challenges and the increasing international competition. The major weaknesses are limited R&D capability abd design innovation, low productivity, high capital investment requirement, process capabilities, finishing, safety features, costs, maintenance and operation, marketing and after sales services. There is a need for huge collaboration with global companies so that it could increase competition and a move to adopt total quality management practices.

Human Resources and Knowledge Adaptability: Talent is a crucial factor in implementing any strategy. Talent management is a critical factor for the manufacturer, especially because the demand for qualified labour is more than the supply. In India, manufacturers have to compete with the big IT firms for white collar employees. Attracting, developing and retaining the talent is difficult the world over and is now being difficult in India as well.

Therefore, it is always necessary to upgrade the man-power skills in technical and techno-managerial dimension.

In a labor-surplus economy, new and efficient technologies are discouraged unless there are sufficient redeployment opportunities.

Service Sector and IT: India's IT industry has flourished with minimum intervention from the Central Government. For starting new IT companies the Indian industry did not face major intervention whereas other industries faced major interventions from the government right from the certification till the establishment. Only, IT industries faced limited labour restrictions on hours and overtime and received foreign investment for it's development. Whether the Indian Government consciously did not regulate IT or only underestimated it's possible growth is unclear but it's growth has been helped by the government as compared to other companies.

B. Demographic

These are outcomes of changes in or changing attitude towards the characteristics of population such as age, gender, ethic, origin, race, sexual orientation and social class. Like the other forces, it presents managers with opportunities and threats and can have major implications for organisations. There are many factors responsible for the change into their composition like labour force, social mobility, education, evolving social and political climate in the countries.

With the result, higher skills and educational requirements has made visible the traditional distinction between manual and non-manual workers. Employees are seeking and demanding parity in employee's benefits among different categories and levels. Earlier, women has been recruited mainly as labour in agriculture and related traditional industries like plantations etc. now they increasingly occupying white collar and managerial positions.

C. Socio-cultural

These are the pressures emanating from the social structure of a country or society or from the national culture. Social structure is the arrangement of relationship between individuals and groups in a society. Societies differ substantially in social structure. In societies that have a high degree of social stratification, there are many distinctions among individuals and groups. The socio-cultural dimensions of the environment consists of factors like customs, life styles and values that characterize the society in which the firms operates and it influences the firms to obtain it's resources, makes its goods and services and function within the society. Population changes, rising educational levels, norms, values and attitudes towards social responsibility are examples of socio-cultural variables.

Population Changes: The changes in population have many consequences for organisations. As, the total population changes, the demand for products and services also change. For example, the decline in the birthrate and improvement in healthcare have increased the average age of the population in the United States. Many firms that marketed their products toward youths are developing the product lines so that it may appeal to an older market. Firms are developing the product lines so that it may appeal to an older market. Firms are developing strategies that will allow them to capitalise on the aging population.

Rising Educational Levels: The rising educational levels enables people to earn more than otherwise also, the increased expectations of workers and the job mobility. If there income is more naturally they can purchase additional goods and services and it will support to raise the overall standard of living of a large segment of the population. Now, workers are not accepting undesirable working conditions that were a generations ago with the workers.

Norms and Values: Norms (standard accepted forms of behaviour) and values (aptitudes toward right and wrong) differ across time and between geographical area. Lifestyles differ among different ethnic groups. Examples, customers expect increasing quality in products.

Social Responsibility: A business or individual should strive to improve the welfare of the society. Norms and values what is considered socially responsible for behaviour that changes over time. During the early part of the twentyfirst century prominent social values and human rights were environmental quality (most prominent, recycling and waste reduction) in addition to general social welfare.

Stakeholders are anyone with a stake in the organisation existence. They think to incorporate socially responsible issue into a firms strategies. To maximise the return to stakeholders decision may be taken to close an unprofitable plant.

D. Politico-legal

These result from political and legal developments within society and significantly affect managers and organisations. The legal environment defines what organisations cannot do at a particular point of time.

Attitudes Towards Business: If the government has pro business attitude then it enables firm to enter into business practices. Smoking and it's related risks alters the public's attitude. So limiting to smoking to workplace or designated area is a necessity to bring changes in the organisation.

Legislation: In India various laws and acts, formulated and amended over the years like—Trade Union Act (1926), The Industrial Employment (Standing Order) Act (1957), Payment of wages Act (1946), The Factories Act (1948), Payment of Gratuity Act(1972) etc. have shaped and tuned the spirit of Indian Organisations and the workforce. The legal environment is becoming more complex and affecting businesses more directly. It has become difficult for businesses to take action without encountering a law, regulation or legal problem.

Levels of Government Influence: Government policies and programmes affect the way market operates. Regulation concerning to many business practices differ between the states and the tax rates vary widely.

Government may provide incentives to attract business to the area, may build industrial parks, service roads and provide low interest bonds to encourage a desirable business to move into the community.

E. Technological

Technological forces are outcomes of changes in the technology that managers use to design, produce or distribute goods and services. Technological innovations bring changes because they are not just changes in the way the work is performed. Instead, the innovation process promotes associated changes in the work relationships and organization structures. Sophisticated information technology is also making organisations more responsive. The team approach adopted by many organisations lead to flatter structures, decentralised decision-making and a more open communication among the leaders and team members.

Demand: Changing technology affects the demand for a firm's product and services, it's production processes and raw materials. It can change the lifestyle and buying patterns of consumers. Recent developments in the field of microcomputers have created opportunities for businesses to engage in business via Internet. Earlier computers were used only by large organisations to handle data processing needs, now personal computers are being used by smaller firms and individuals that was not imagined fifteen years ago. Similarly, new developments in technology have reduced prices of computers and expanded to the general public rather than to business, scientific and professional users.

Technology has removed certain products from the market. A number of chemicals that have been used by farmers to control insets or plants that are prohibited from use or require licensure as a consequence of those chemicals appearing the food chain.

Production Process: Technology also changes production methods. Example—robotics, represents one of the most visible challenges to the existing production methods.

When production was first automated, some workers were displaced, new jobs were created to maintain the automated equipment.

Evaluating Technological Changes: Technology, represents both, potential threats and potential opportunities for the established products. Products with new technology are often introduced but it is hard to assess their market potential. When ballpoint pens were first introduced they leaked, skipped and left large blotches of ink on the writing surface. Fountain pen manufacturers believed that new technology was not a threat to existing products and can't attempt to produce ball-point pens until substantial market share of fountain pen could be lost.

It is quite difficult to predict the impact of new technology on an existing product, still the need to monitor the environment for new technological developments is obvious.

MODEL QUESTIONS

1. Analyse the environment of Human Resource Management.
2. What factors have hindered the progress of Human Resource Management?
3. What has resulted with socio-cultural factors in the society?

Chapter

3

Emerging Role of Human Resources

CONCEPT

Human Resource is one of the most complex and challenging fields of modern management. Successful management of an organisation's human resources is an exciting, dynamic and challenging field, especially at a time when companies are globalising larger numbers of knowledge workers.

It is concerned with human problems of an organisation so that individuals could contribute maximum for accomplishment of common goals and at the same time attain social satisfaction as well as objectives of each could be accomplished.

Success of an organisation depends upon the quality of HR. Hence, acquiring and retaining good human resources is a precondition for any organisation to be effective and efficient.

HRM is a process with four functions like—acquiring, developing, motivating and retaining human resources. These four functions and their constituent sub-functions have changed over the years due to changes in the social and political environment of business and as a result of new development in the management thought.

In order to exhibit a shared mindset the HR practitioners must be willing to undertake change and a self realisation that change is essential in the process. Because, the self realisation is the process to stimulate the new role.

New roles and competencies in HRM must be acquired to add value to the organisations. The importance of HRM competencies and knowledge as a leverage cannot be understated. Because, HRM competencies in literature are understood, such as: (*i*) good business understanding; (*ii*) shared mindset between HRM and the rest by the organisation; (*iii*) strategic thinking capability; (*iv*) response to change and the ability to act accordingly; and (*v*) movement towards customisation of HR products and services.

So far as employment stability is concerned, it does not provide any implication to the strategy of human resources management due to reasons of unionisation, specialisation and corporatisation of the organisations in the early 1990s. The strategic HRM is actively adopted as a means of meeting the challenges placed on the traditional public service culture which has been enshrined within the organisation. The HRM practitioners have to be effective in balancing their different roles. They are required to be strategic business partners to line managers, deliver HR products and services and provide consultancy to line managers.

ROLE OF HUMAN RESOURCES IN THE BUSINESS ENVIRON-MENT OF NEXT MILLENNIUM

The role of human resources in a new dimension of business is to be redefined as because management is the important resource which is basic to most achievement. It is the normal outgrowth of management maturing and management skill and knowledge. It is a means toward achievement and is fundamental in our efforts to progress. The knowledge of management and it's skill are now recognised as an important resource of any nation. There are lack of proper management in nations but they are not underdeveloped nations. The trend toward more involvement of human resources with management plus experience in utilising human resource management will accelerate the concept of human resource as the basic resource. The emphasis on human resource management as a resource will solve our problems as a means.

In this context, human resources have to do a strategic analysis of the changes taking place in the business environment to build organizational capacity to maximise the potential of the business in the market place. So, this emphasis on end results will stimulate values, philosophy and the cultures in which we operate. Though their role in the past held a pivotal but there will be their critical role in the next century as we move forward. Because, their role is recognised from administrative to strategic business partner in respect of diverse workforce as well as changes in the environment.

HUMAN RESOURCES EVOLUTION

The human resources professional always worked to improve working conditions business practices, job satisfaction and workers productivity. They have made tremendous contribution to the free enterprise system. Though, the activities of human resources are involved from the beginning of the 20th century to the date which has been explained below for greater changes in the nature of job of human resources professionals and their role in organsiational growth and development.

History of Human Resource Management

There is a vast difference between HRM and the personnel management. During 1990s a great change in the nature and scope of personnel management was observed. Functions of personnel management not only involve labour welfare, industrial relations and physical administration but also developing relationship with the employees on long-term basis and treating employees as a part of the organisation. Hence, the American Society for Personnel Administration supported to change its name to as Human Resource Management. Over the past eighty years, the scientific management approach and the human relations approach appeared and then disappeared too. But, later on human resource approach has acquired prominence.

Scientific Management Approach

In 1911, F. W. Taylor wrote the principles of Scientific management so he was considered "Father of scientific Management". In 1878, he began to experiment an engineer and inventor with new managerial concepts while being employed at the Midvale Steel Co. At. Midvale, his rise from labourer to Chief Engineer within 6 years of period gave him the opportunity to tackle work shirking problem. According to him, employees deliberately worked slower than their capabilities. He advocated the solution of right people for right jobs, training them adequately, placing them in jobs according to their suitability and remunerating them handsomely.

Taylor considered that through time and motion study it is possible to fix a standard time for doing a particular task. To encourage workers to complete the work within the standard time, he recommended two price rates. If a man performs the work within or less than the standard time he should be paid a higher price rate. If he does not complete the work within the standard time, he should be given a lower price rate. For example, if the standard production has been fixed for 8 units/day for 8 hr, the higher price rate for 8 units or more may be Rs 8 per unit while the lower price rate to less than 8 units may be 80/unit.

The scientific management approach resulted in work methods and techniques that emphasised employees output.

Personnel departments of big manufacturing organisations have been responsible for recruiting, selecting and training staff and ensuring their health and safety. Also, personnel departments of many big companies supported welfare programs like job training, company housing, employees loans, insurance plans and recreational programmes. However, such practices were not very successful in bringing about *behavioural changes* and *productivity gains* desired by the management. That is why the employee welfare programs became less popular during

1920s and 1930s. hence, the personal departments of big organisations were interested to implement scientific management techniques.

Human Relations Approach

The Hawthorne studies conducted during 1930s and 1940s, forced the organisations to shift attention from scientific management approach to human relations approach. The results of these studies suggested that employees productivity was affected not only by the way the job was designed for the economic rewards but also by certain social and psychological factors. Although the human relations approach was instrumental in improving the work environment for many workers, it was not very successful in improving their productivity and job satisfaction due to many reasons. During the 1950s and 1960s, the human relations approach began to be seen as outdated, and was abandoned by many organisations.

Human Resources Approach

In 1970s, research in behavioural sciences suggested not to treat people as factors of production only but also as resources or human beings who act on the basis of emotions alone.The human resources approach is based on principles like :

- Employees are assets to an organisation.
- Policies, programmes and practices must help employees in their work and personal development.
- It is necessary to create and maintain environment conducive to work

IMPLICATIONS OF CHANGES WITH HUMAN RESOURCES MANAGEMENT PRACTICES

Organisation's effort for new decorations, office furnishing, space utilisation and facility provisions will make employees more laborious and healthy and this environment will be conducive to their working. The work related health problems will also be reduced to a great extent by managers.

Employee rights will have the same trend in the future too. As the employer's right to lay off workers will be constrained by law, it will create complexities for human resources manager.

In spite of decreasing trend in unions the anonymity between the management and workers will increase on the basis of determination between the educated professionals and minimum wage service earners.

Working from home computers will cause a major restructuring in pay levels. The companies will have to determine the potential of each job and pay accordingly. As different individuals working at home may also expect from an organization to implement new quality control steps, close supervision of work will not be a possibility. So, monitoring techniques will have to be developed for ensuring accuracy and punctuality in work culture.

With organisations dehiring employees, sense of commitment and loyalty to organization is likely to suffer tremendously because employees may become more self-oriented.

Due to growing importance of human resource management, senior executives in the organisation will be coming up from human resource management function. In future, it is expected that ambitious executives will employ human resource management to promote executives to the top instead of keeping them involved in traditional functions like engineering, production, finance or marketing.

Competition among companies for the skilled workers will shoot up. Companies will rely only on higher learning institutions. This will increase tension between high and low wage earners. Therefore, motivating low wage service worker through employees participation and non-financial rewards will be a great challenge.

The major implication for the future is likely to be the injection of constitutional rights of citizenship within the employing organisation that will help to reduce feelings of helplessness. The gradual movement towards job enrichment would boost confidence of employees and reduce feelings of meaninglessness. Development of viable primary work groups will reduce impression of lack of norms. In view of this, human resource manager must look for approaches that will more effectively integrate human and organisational values.

In conclusion, the post-reforms period can be called as generating more employment opportunities and higher standards of living. Greater change in workers' profile regarding age, gender, religion, region, caste, language, culture, ethnicity and education will be needed for creative and flexible work environment. The flexible work arrangements which include telecommuting, flexible time schedules, virtual office, alternative work week, work at home, compressed work week and voluntary reduced hours will be helpful in establishing a new global work culture.

For such greater changes organisations go for a stable and flatter structure. Managers are acting as facilitators and workers are going to be partners in industry. They will be driven by intrinsic values. Loyalty has been replaced by competence and employees are empowered to take decisions and have greater degree of autonomy. The latest communication tools like email, fax, pagers and Internet technologies have totally revolutionised the work atmosphere in terms of time and space.

So, human resource professionals have to convince the top management about the importance of 'human resources'. They have to achieve organisational goals through development of human resources emphasising on functional knowledge and diagnostic skill, strong self concept, personal influence, tactical planning and result orientation. This will create a capable and multi-skilled workforce aligned with human resources strategies through training, education and development programs.

MODEL QUESTIONS

1. Describe the evolution of human resource management.
2. Briefly discuss the implications of changes in vistas of technology, environment and people.

Chapter

4

Introduction to Training and Development

CONCEPT

Initially, the training was limited to technical training only. But, due to increasing competition commercial organisations realised a need for management training as well because of the complexities involved in the management of large organisations.

In the mid-1940s, it was first adopted by large commercial organisations in the west as part of their regular commercial acitivity. Thus, western companies created formal training groups in their organisational structure.

It is a collection of actions, which enables the organisation to achieve its goals. Its need can be identified by deducting the existing skills from the job requirements.

It is the systematic development of knowledge, skills and attitudes required to perform a given task or job successfully in an individual. It includes:

- To identifying the training needs of the individual
- To design the suitable training programme to eliminate the gaps in knowledge, skill or attitude.
- To conduct the training programme.
- To evaluate the effectiveness of the training programme and making necessary changes.

If Fills the Gap Between

- What someone can do?
- What someone will the able to do ?

It makes us aware with the rules and procedures to guide the behavior of the employees and with the help of that improve the performance of employees on present job and prepares them for taking up new assignments in future.

Scope of Training

During the past few years, the scope and application of training has been widened. It is like a key tool for increasing organisational effectiveness and job-related performance. Now it's value is acknowledged in making behavioural changes, developing life skills and resulting in personal growth. It equips an individual with the competencies that help him to cope with day-to-day problems of living and managing interpersonal relations and improving his interpersonal effectiveness. It has influenced every facet of an individual's life. As a result of these developments now human relation and personal development training has a significant place in the cycle of training.

OBJECTIVES OF TRAINING

The objectives of training are:

- to impart the basic knowledge and skill to the new entrants and enable t hem to perform their jobs well.
- to equip the employees to meet the changing requirements of the job and the organisation.
- to teach the employees the new techniques and ways of performing the jobs or operations.
- to prepare the employees for higher level tasks and build up a second line of competent managers.

There are three elements of training objectives. Outcomes of the training programme means observable behaviour required at the end of the training, conditions of the training programme means clear outcomes should take place and standards of the training programme means expected level attainment in terms of quantity, quality, accuracy relevant to the job.

ASSUMPTIONS OF TRAINING

The syllabus is developed quickly and discussed with other officers of the organisation. To start a course (minimum qualification is needed) *ie certain academic qualification and* many years of experience.

As soon as the first batch leaves, the next batch arrives because there are many people to train and time is short. After the first round or two, the syllabus is standardised and a new training programme is established and standardised across provinces or the whole system.

The underlying/basic assumptions for this kind of process are usually not stated because there is no time'. But, it can be developed and checked against experience and more useful assumptions can be developed.

PURPOSES OF TRAINING

The need for the training of employees become clear form the observations made by the different authorities.

Increasing Productivity

A good human performance often leads to increased operational productivity and company profit.

Improving Quality

A well planned training results in quality improvement that may be in relationship to a company; product or service, or in reference to the intangible organisational employment atmosphere.

Help a Company to Fulfill Its Future Personnel Needs

Organisation that have an internal education programme makes less drastic manpower change and adjustments due to sudden personnel alterations.

Improve Organisational Climate

Through a planned training programme supervisory pressure decrease and internal promotions become stressed. Moreover, product quality improve; financial incentives and base pay rates increase.

It improves managerial mental states if supervisors know that they can better themselves through development programmes designed by the company. A good training prevents industrial accidents.

Obsolescence Prevention

A sound training programme helps to prevent manpower obsolescence and develops creativity also helps to take initiative and which may be due to age, temperament or motivation, or the inability of a person to adapt himself to technological changes.

Personal Growth

It provides the participants an awareness, skill, altruistic philosophy and make possible personal growth.

The need for training arises because of the following reasons:

(*i*) Employment of new, inexperience or contract labour requires detailed instruction for an effective performance of a job;

(*ii*) To reduce grievance and minimising accident rates;

(*iii*) To enable the old employees to keep abreast of the changing methods, techniques and use of sophisticated tools and equipment;

(*iv*) To maintain the validity of an organisation as a whole and raising the morale of its employees;

(*v*) To reduce learning time, reduce supervision time, reduce waste and spoilage of raw material and produce quality goods and develop their potential.

A training programme is essential for the purpose of meeting the specific problems of a particular organisation like—changes in design, volume of business, the demands of competition and economy, the quality of materials processed, individual adjustments, promotions and career development

FUNCTIONS OF TRAINING

According to Miller, training involves the following five functions:

(i) ***Analysis:*** It helps in identify the training needs and specifying the behavioural objectives.

(ii) ***Development:*** It prepares necessary teaching material and specific methods so that effective learning may occur.

(iii) ***Operation:*** It helps in the selection of suitable training methods and identifying the required training aids. It also helps in the smooth functioning of a training programme.

(iv) ***Evaluation:*** It monitors the effectiveness of the trainers in meeting their goals, success of programmes and the organisational impact of training.

According to *Prof. John Mee,* the work of training should be done at two levels, like :

(*i*) The training department should assume the primary responsibility of trainers in teaching areas :

- for formal orientation
- for the training of supervisors in human relation
- for the development of executives for co-operative education in schools and colleges
- for the general education of employees.

(*ii*) Line supervisors and employees should carry the bulk of teaching load in the following areas:

- on-the-job instruction to employees
- instruction in the technical and professional aspects of a business

- daily development of superiors and executives through counselling
- departmental communication and staff meetings as part of an overall training programme

BENEFITS OF TRAINING

It makes the employee more productive and more useful to an organisation.

Benefits to the Business

(*i*) Trained workers can work more efficiently with machines, tool, and materials.

(*ii*) There are less chances of accidents.

(*iii*) Training improves the knowledge of employees regarding the use of machines and equipment.

(*iv*) Trained workers requires less supervision, as they know how to handle operation properly and can show superior performance.

(*v*) They can turn our better quality goods by putting the materials, tools and equipment to use.

Benefits to the Employees

(*i*) It makes employees more loyal, useful, efficient and effective for an organisation.

(*ii*) By combining materials, tools and machines with confidence. They can produce more with minimum effort and can secure promotions.

(*iii*) Enables employees to move from one organisation to another easily.

(*iv*) Contributes to higher production, fewer mistakes, greater job satisfaction and lower labor turnover. Also enable employees to cope with organisational, social and technological change.

TRAINING AND EDUCATION

Although, training and education aims to enhance learning but they are used for different purposes. Training is concerned with increase in the knowledge and skill of an employee for doing a particular job where as education is concerned with increase in general knowledge and understanding of the total environment. It is person oriented. Training is generally conducted by the business organisations in which the job is located but education is imparted through schools and colleges.

Though, training and education differ in nature and orientation. But, they are complementary to each other. There is some education in all training and in all education there is some training

TRAINING AND DEVELOPMENT

Training

It is the systematic development of knowledge, skills and attitudes required to perform a given task or job successfully in an individual. It includes:

- Identifying the training needs of the individual
- Designing the suitable training programme to eliminate the gaps in knowledge, skill or attitude.
- Conducting the training programme.
- Evaluating the effectiveness of the training programme and making necessary changes.

It fills the gap between

What someone can do?

What someone would be able to do?

It makes us aware with the rules and procedures to guide the behaviour of the employee and with the help of that improve the performance of employees on present job and prepares them for taking up new assignments in future.

Development

It provides people to do better in existing job and prepares them for greater responsibilities in future.

It builts on strength and helps to overcome the weaknesses and also ensures that the organisation has the expertise it needs to achieve the strategic objective.

Some Important Aspects of Development

Learning is a continuous process. It aims at assimilating and understanding those processes and devising ways that lead to better job-performance.

One must realise that there is always a scope for learning and improvement. The potentialities of the employees should be properly utilised and opportunities must be provided for the development of employees.

Development provides opportunities, to rise to the occasion and use their qualities. In normal work life, problems, difficulties, challenges and other like situations help in the development of the hidden potentials in the employees.

In the process of development, similar to training, the appraisal of past and present performance is necessary. So, the participation of the employees is also beneficial in identifying the strengths and weaknesses of the training and development.

MODEL QUESTIONS

1. Explain training and its purpose.
2. What are the assumptions of training?
3. Focus on training functions.
4. What is the distinction between training and education?
5. What is the distinction between training and development?

Chapter 5 Training and Training Needs Assessment

TRAINING NEED ASSESSMENT/ANALYSIS

A *'Training Needs Assessment'*, or *'Training Needs Analysis'*, is a method which determines whether a training need exists and if it does, what training is required to fill the gap.

The results of training needs analysis highlights the subject matter that needs to be covered during the training course. Afterwards, the knowledge and skills gained during the training course increase the abilities and allow the participants to perform their jobs at an acceptable level. For example, when a new information system is introduced, it is assumed that no one has the knowledge to operate it and so the training need may not be obvious.

Purpose of Training Need Assessment

If training need assessment is done correctly, it ensures the solution and addresses the real issues and focuses on the appropriate resources, time and effort toward the targeted solutions. The reasons for doing training need assessment are:

- to determine whether training is needed
- to determine causes of poor performance
- to determine content and scope of training
- to determine desired training outcomes

- to provide a basis of measurement
- to gain management support

Levels of Training Needs Assessment

There are three levels of training needs assessment:

(*i*) Individual analysis

(*ii*) Organisational analysis

(*iii*) Task analysis

Individual Analysis: It analyses that how well the individual employee is doing the job and examines that what kind of training which employee needs.

Sources of information to conduct individual analysis are:

(*i*) *Performance evaluation:* It identifies weaknesses and areas of improvement.

(*ii*) *Performance problems:* The issues related to— accidents, grievances, productivity, absenteeism, product quality, equipment utilisation, customer complaints etc.

(*iii*) *Observation:* It means behaviour and the results of the behaviour.

(*iv*) *Work samples:* It observes the products generated.

(*v*) *Interviews:* Discuss with manager, supervisor and employee and ask employee about what they believe and what they need to learn.

(*vi*) *Questionnaires:* It is the written form of the interview, tests, must measure the job-related qualities such as job knowledge and skills.

(*vii*) *Attitude surveys:* It measures morale, motivation and satisfaction.

(*viii*) *Checklists or training progress charts:* This indicates the up-to-date listing of current skills.

Organisational Analysis: It observes the effectiveness of the organisation and finds out where and under what conditions the training may be conducted. It identifies issues like—

- impacts on environment and on operating costs.
- state of the economy and increasing global marketplaces.
- changing work force demographics and changing technology and automation.
- organisational goals (like how effective is the organisation in meeting its goals), resources available (like money, facilities—materials on hand and current, available expertise within the organisation).
- climate and support for training and sexual harassment and workplace violence.

Sources of information to conduct organisation analysis are:

1. Organisation goals, objectives, mission statements and strategic plans.
2. Staffing inventory, succession planning, long-and short-term staffing needs.
3. Changes in equipment, technology or automation, long and short-term needs, labour/management relationships, grievances, turnover rates, absenteeism, suggestions, productivity, accidents, short-term sickness, attitude surveys, customer complaints.
4. Analysis of efficiency indices, costs of labour, materials and distribution, quality of products, equipment utilisation, production rates, waste, down time, late deliveries repairs.
5. Annual report and planning systems.
6. Plans for reorganisation.
7. Audit exceptions, reward systems.
8. Employee attitudes and satisfaction.

Task Analysis: It provides data about a job or a group of jobs and the knowledge, skills, attitudes and abilities needed to achieve optimum performance.

Sources of information to conduct task analysis are as follows:

(*i*) *Job description:* It describes different aspects of a job such as the tasks involved, the responsibilities of the job and the derivable. Also the setting and the work environment of the job. It is used in recruitment, training, performance appraisal, wage and salary administration.

(*ii*) *KSA analysis:* It is list of specified tasks for each job including knowledge, skills, attitudes and abilities required of the job holder.

(*iii*) *Performance standards:* It is the standards by which employees will be judged and it is needed to identify performance discrepancies.

(*iv*) *Job inventory questionnaire:* It evaluates the tasks in terms of importance and the time spent in performing.

(*v*) *Review literature about the job:* Research the 'best practices' from other companies and review professional journals.

(*vi*) *Analysis of operating problems:* The problems such as down time, waste, repairs, late deliveries, quality control.

Process of Training Needs Assessment

Training need assessment process consists of three steps namely: performing GAP analysis, prioritising the needs and developing the action plan.

Performing 'Gap' Analysis: The first step in the training need assessment process is to identify the problem needs then to find out the causes of these needs in the organisational context. The gap analysis is performed to identify the need of an employee.

Prioritising the Needs: The result of gap analysis are discussed with employer and prioritisation of needs is done on the basis of importance in the organisation. The report is prepared based on the discussion.

Developing Action Plan: To design a training programme, training manager sets the objectives, identify suitable training methodology, identify resource person, estimate the cost for the training programme, and finalise the dates to the training programme.

Techniques Involved in Organisational and Personal Needs

The training manager, prioritises the training, based on the urgency of the need, the extent of the need (how many employees need to be trained) and the resources available. To identify the need of training, it is not possible for the training manager to adopt one training need assessment technique. Hence, he adopts two or more training need assessment techniques such as—

(*i*) Direct observation and Questionnaires.

(*ii*) Consultation with persons in key positions, and/or with specifie knowledge.

(*iii*) Review of relevant literature.

(*iv*) Interviews.

(*v*) Focus groups.

(*vi*) Tests, records, report studies and work samples.

(*vii*) Behavioural Anchored Rating Scale (BARS)

Advantages of Training Needs Assessment

Following are the advantages of training needs assessment.

(*i*) It explains that which type of skills are important to job performance. Not only from the point of view of the job holders, but also from the point of view of their managers as well.

(*ii*) It helps to identify which skill are actually aligned with organisational goals and in-turn related to the reward system of an organisation.

(*iii*) It indicates to identify the critical skills that are needed for training.

(*iv*) It gives a consensus without the alignment of rewards and incentives.

COMPETENCY MAPPING

It can be used in self and multi-rater assessments in identifying the areas of strength and the need for improvement.

These are identified behaviours, knowledge, skills and abilities that directly and positively impact the success of employees and the organisation. It can be measured, enhanced, and improved through coaching and employee development opportunities. There are some examples of core competency as—

(*i*) *Technical and functional expertise:* These are hidden knowledge and skills, described in observable and measurable terms that are necessary to perform a particular type or level of work activity. It reflects a career-long experience in the job or occupational area.

(*ii*) *Understanding the business:* Understanding the organization's purpose and mission.

(*iii*) *Achieving results:* Attaining goals and objectives.

(*iv*) *Serving the customer:* Fulfilling the needs of internal and external customers.

(*v*) *Teamwork:* Collaborate and cooperate to get the job done.

(*vi*) *Interpersonal and communication skills:*

(*a*) *Interpersonal:* Develop and maintain positive relationships.

(*b*) *Communication:* Exchanging ideas and opinions.

(*vii*) Leadership and personal effectiveness:

(*a*) *Leadership:* Motivate, influence and support others to accomplish team and organisational goals.

(b) *Personal Effectiveness:* Develop oneself, achieve results and solve problems. plan, organise and manage own time and work.

Apart from the discussed core competencies, it is necessary for every organisation to know whether—

- the employees are involved in the right direction.
- the effectiveness requires what skills and knowledge in a job.
- the skills and knowledge of the employee is suitable or requires some kind of training.
- the job expectations has any link with the culture and strategy of the organisation. For the performance improvement of an employee the competency model is designed to find answers to these questions.

Competency Model

A competency Model is a descriptive tool that identifies the skills, knowledge and attitude of an employee to perform effectively a role in the organisation and help the business to meet its strategic objectives.

The model is presented as a learning continuum. Its lists the relevant skills or competencies for each level of employees in an organisation as a learning continuum and is divided into three levels *viz.* basic, intermediate and advanced level.

Basic Level: This indicates the level at which someone new to a skill or area performs.

Intermediate Level: A level at which someone with detailed knowledge in an area performs. It is expected that the person is capable of taking operational responsibility for an area.

Advanced Level: At this level the person is in the highest ranking official in the organisation. But, it may also describe a lower ranking official with specialized knowledge in a subject area.

The competency approach provides a better guide to–

(*i*) Reduce the ambiguities in job and work expectations.

(*ii*) Hire the best available people and maximise productivity.

(*iii*) Enhance 360 degree feedback processes.

(*iv*) Align behaviour with organisational strategies and values adapt to change.

Implementing the Competency Model

The person and the team responsible for implementing this competency model desires—

(*i*) The support from the management to carry out the entire study.

(*ii*) To identify the competencies and create a model of competency based performance.

(*iii*) The improvement in organisations.

(*iv*) To know how to use the individual competency based assessment, analysis and planning in a competency based format.

(*v*) To know how to implement the individual development plans.

(*vi*) Designing and developing the competency based learning in intervals.

(*vii*) Learning strategies and medium for competency based intervals.

Competency Assessment Tool (CAT)

It assesses one's current professional competencies and calculates the skills gaps on providing data. *Example:* where you are now and where you want to go and also makes recommendations on how to get there. It is programmed to handle the individuals who are currently in industry and wish to remain there or for those planning to get a position an industry.

Each competency model contains professional competencies arranged in four categories. They are—

- Personal attributes
- Leadership qualities
- Expertise
- Specific Skills

The personal attribute and leadership qualities addresses the competencies that is relevant to all, regardless of any discipline, that is why all are benefited to take the self-assessment exam.

While person's expertise and their specific skills helps in career and advancement.

The Competency Assessment Tool is a basis for assessment and career planning. It provides a list of competencies that is relevant to one's progress.

(*i*) It helps to evaluate the proficiency level in their competencies.

(*ii*) It allows to target specific competencies for development.

(*iii*) It suggests a variety of traditional and non-traditional learning activities to develop the required competencies.

MODEL QUESTIONS

1. Describe training need and its purpose.
2. Discuss levels of training needs assessment.
3. What are the process of training needs assessment?
4. Write notes on competency model and competency assessment tool.

Chapter

6 Training Strategy

ISSUES OF A TRAINING PROGRAMME

A well designed training strategy is designed to distribute the learning into manageable 'learning units'. Training strategy can be defined as—a style of training interaction suitable to a particular trainee specified by the execution of similar training plan.

There are many strategic issues to be considered while designing a training programme. Out of which four basic strategic issues to overcome the training programmes are as follows:

Goals setting: The training system works only on those goals which can help to attain, and which are adequately backed by organisational contributions. There are a few points to be considered as—*firstly,* whether the training programme under consideration is realistic in the need of a particular organisation and in the general context of its development; *secondly,* the usefulness of training programme and *thirdly,* the selection of particular programmes and of suitable people for them.

Action perspectives: The training is a systematic attempt in action perspective to develop the human resources—individual, group and organisation to manage some present tasks and situations as well as those in the future. An effective training strategy the trainers role from traditional in structure to change agent and system consultant to the organisation.

Planning the specifications: The training particulars worked out by the training system and agreed by the work organisation includes services and activities. And this is required to be carried out by the participants' after their return from the training programme.

GENERAL PHILOSOPHY AND CONCEPT OF TRAINING

General equipment of knowledge and system of working need an overall concept that defines the objective of training for attaining an organisation objective. This specification of general concept is modality that embraces varied training methods and procedures. For implementing a modality, an organisation can prescribe varied methods. The selected modality contains frame for designing and sequentially arranging training programmes, deciding their contents, and shortlisting the methods to achieve the desired results.

The training system can be

- direct contact or distance training
- formal or non-formal learning
- centralised or dispersed and
- content or process modalities.

Direct Contact or Distance Training: The trainers and learners are face to face in direct contact-training programmes. It limits the number of participants in a programme. Distance training responds to train a large number of people. It also keeps people on the job, let them learn at their own pace and simplify the requirements for different organisations to collaborate in training. The electronic technologies have made the distance learning highly attractive. It prepares a series of modules to be used by an individual or small group of participants as learning experiences.

Formal or Non-formal Learning: The formal training programme is a training that follows some designed form. In systematic, formal training each phase of the process produces results needed to the next phase.

It also includes careful assessment to determine training goals, designing and building methods and materials that are directly aligned to achieve goals and implement training. In the informal modalities emphasis is on conscious, guided experiences.

Centralised and Dispersed: In a centralized model, one institute is responsible for planning programmes, staffing and funding them, ensuring that everything is according to the standard and often selecting the participants. This pattern is common in developing countries with sufficient training resources in one or two central institutes but provide training in many places. The central institute initiates, guides and support all aspects of.

The dispersed model is the networks of autonomous training unit, which are responsible for its own training plans and programmes. It helps the participants to choose their own training programme and also their own field for training.

Content or Process Modalities—Six Orientations: The training strategies vary depending on the learning outcomes the participants seek to achieve. At one end, training for new or improved proficiency, have different training strategy for different purpose. At the other end, process learning such as teamwork or leadership, eagerness and ability to mobilize organisational support for a plane innovation, or a more effective consultant-client relationship have different training strategy.

The Academic Orientation

The academic orientation is not confined to academic institutions only. It is commonly used in many training activities, where specific improvements are expected to take place on the job and in the orientation.

This type of orientation makes two assumptions. *First,* content and understanding can be passed on effectively by those who have knowledge. *Second,* participants capable to translate abstract generalisations in concrete situations.

The Laboratory Orientation

Laboratory orientation gives importance to the process and not to the content.It is useful to provide suitable place to its purpose and possible to help people to examine their inner reality, in order to better understand the sources of their behaviour and that of others, and to become aware that these are important factors in actual performance on the job.

The Activity Orientation

This orientation puts training on the job and avoids the problems of transfer from training back to the job. The theories of activity orientation is the ability of the participants to do the particular job the way in which the organisation operates. And the production and training may be combined in a very simple way.

The Action Orientation

Its focus is on process, not on content. Due to lack of practice in training, action soon fails in quality, and discontinues in many cases. It ensures neither sound practice nor the understanding of working procedures required for further developments.

The Person Development Orientation

During the programme participants work on the task and problems similar to those faced on the job. Also, they analyse and explain the factors underlying the experiences they have undergone, and the points of view with which they approached them.

The Organisation Development Orientation

The organisation development orientation incorporates two provisions to minimise discrepancies between individual and organisational interests. One is prior involvement of individuals in organisational changes. The second is that such discrepancies may occur and may lead to shifting of some staff within the organisation.

TRAINING OBJECTIVES

There are some points to consider in the training objective :

- it is performance-based.
- it is clear to the trainees what is expected from them and how they will be tested.
- the shift and responsibility for learning is upon the trainees themselves.
- the end-result is observable and measurable.

TRAINING DESIGN

A Training design is a detailed plan that what you will do, why you will do and the best ways to reach your training objectives.

The steps involved in designing the training programme are :

(*i*) to select a combination of strategies and break the general training objectives into constituent parts.

(*ii*) to use the specifications of different training methods to arrive at a rough grand total of time and facilities required by the programme as a whole.

(*iii*) to decide on the different packages in which the programme could be offered.

(*iv*) to work the detailed training events into training sequences and finally into the shape of the total programme package.

The design and implementation of training is done by trainer, training institutions, departments and the trainees.

The design of training is a vital part of the systematic approach of training programme. The trainer, design a training programme considering the following:

(*i*) Use available resources efficiently collaborate with a variety of client organisation to meet their requirements

(*ii*) Training is suitable to meet identified training needs.

(*iii*) Ensure a satisfactory outcome form the training.

While designing training two things are essential to know first, know how many people need to be trained and their location. Without this we may design the training program for a few when there are many to be trained, or provide training at an inconvenient location which results in unnecessary expense and loss of it.

The second is essential to know the standard of quality required to be achieved by trainees keeping in mind that the higher the standard the higher will be the demand in time and resources needed.

Process of Training Design

The process of training design consists of eight steps that meet the needs of participants and trainers. This model includes the following steps which can be applied to a variety of training formats, including face-to-face, online, interactive and satellite-based trainings.

Define Purpose of the Training and Target Audience: The first step to design a training programme is to be clear about what is needed to complete a training. For some training, purpose and audience is determined by sponsor or well-established professional development needs. Sometimes, trainer need to sort out and prioritize the training needs before determining the focus of training.

Determine Participates Needs

There are several ways to find out the needs and expectations of training participants.

(*i*) Whether participants have completed brief, written survey as part of their registration packet.

(*ii*) Review evaluation and feedback forms from past-related training events.

Define Training Goals and Objectives: To finalise the training goals and objectives of a training program, trainer have to follow the following steps:

(*i*) To clarify the expected outcomes.

(*ii*) To plan the specific training activities

(*iii*) To select/develop materials

(*iv*) To design evaluation procedures.

(*v*) To communicate programme intent to the training participants and others.

(*vi*) Ensuring that the training is realistic and appropriate for the purpose intended

Outline Training Content

Most of the training programmes are divided into three key segments, like—an introduction, a learning component and a final and evaluation complement.

Introduction: The introduction establishes a positive learning environment. It's important to introduce some content in the introductory activities, so that participants experience these activities as meaningful.

Learning Component: During this part of the programme, participants accomplish the training objectives. Concepts and ideas and teaching strategies are practiced and discussed. To be effective, the activities involve participants in acquiring knowledge or practicing skills.

Warp-up and Evaluation Segment: This segment helps to bridge the gap between training and implementation and promote a positive feelings of closure.

Prepare a Written Training Design

A written document provides a detailed plan of the training session including the goals and objectives. Consider the skill, expertise and training style of each of the trainers in making this designation.

Prepare Participant Evaluation Forms

The purpose of the evaluation is to determine the extent to which the training achieved its objectives and to identify what adjustments it needs to be made to the training design or follow-up process.

Determine follow-up Activities for the Event

To be effective, follow-up activities should be planned, and should include opportunities for participants to reflect the content what they learned during the training and the process of implementation.

MODEL QUESTIONS

1. Describe the issues involved in a training programme.
2. Describe modalities in training.
3. Explain content and process modalities.
4. Explain training design and the steps involved in it.
5. Explain the process of training design.

Chapter

7 New Issues in Manpower Training

There are various methods of training which can be broadly classified into—'on-the-job training methods' and 'off-the-job training methods'. The choice of a method depends on different factors like—competence of instructors, programme suitability to the participants, the programme design, the content and its cost.

The methods depend on the objectives of the training, culture of the organisation and the type of knowledge to be offered. To ascertain the effectiveness of the training and its methods evaluation techniques are also available there.

OBJECTIVES OF TRAINING

Training methods have a number of objectives. Some of the important objectives are :

- to equip the employees to meet the changing requirements of the job and the organisation.
- to teach the employees the new techniques and ways of performing the jobs or operations.
- to prepare the employees for higher level tasks and build up a second line of competent managers.

There are three elements of training objectives. Outcomes of the training programme, conditions of the training programme and standards of the training programme.

ASSUMPTIONS OF TRAINING

The syllabus for training is developed quickly and discussed with other officers of the organisation. To start a course a certain academic qualification and many years of experience is needed.

As soon as the first batch leaves, the next batch arrives because there are many people to train and time is short. After the first round or two, the syllabus is standardised and a new training programme is established and standardised across provinces or the whole system.

The basic assumptions for this kind of process are usually not stated because there is no time'. But, it can be developed and checked against experience and more useful assumptions can be developed.

PURPOSES OF TRAINING

The purposes of training are as—

Productivity Enhancement

A good human performance leads to increased operational productivity and company profit.

Quality Improvement

Good works make less operational mistakes. Quality improvement may be in relationship to a company; product or service, or in reference to the intangible organisational employment atmosphere.

Improve Health and Safety

Proper training improves managerial mental states if supervisors know that they can better themselves through development programmes designed by the company.

Obsolescence Prevention

Training and development programmes develops creativity and helps to take initiative and also helps to prevent manpower obsolescence, which may be due to age, temperament or motivation, or the inability of a person to adapt himself to technological changes.

Personal Growth

Management development programmes are a need to meet specific problems and demands of individual career development, job and personnel changes and changes in the volume of business.

The need for training arises because of the following reasons:

(*i*) More use of technology in production.

(*ii*) Need for additional hands to cope with more production of goods and services and to cope grievances.

(*iii*) Employment of new, inexperience or contract labour requires detailed instruction for an effective performance of a job.

(*iv*) Old employees need refresher training to enable them to keep abreast of the changing methods, techniques and use of sophisticated tools and equipment

(*v*) To enable the employees to do the work in amore effective way, to reduce learning time, reduce supervision time, produce quality goods and improve employee morale etc.

FACTORS IN THE SELECTION OF TRAINING METHODS

The responsible factors for the choice of training methods :

Human Factors

Trainer : The trainer must have adequate knowledge of psychology and experience to deal with human problems and to react quickly in discussion. Also, the analytical skills to analyse what participants say in the training programme.

Participants : The important points to be considered from the participants point of view, while selecting the training methods of a training program *i.e.,* his educational background, age, experience etc..

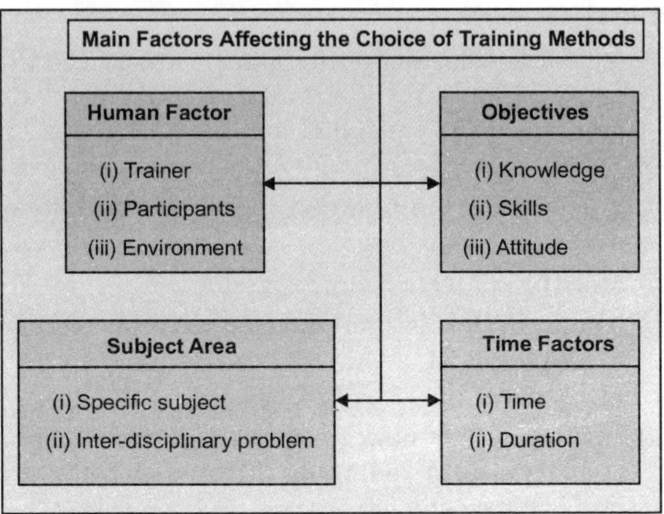

Environment : The choice of method depends on the social and cultural factors in the environment. To manage the environmental factors many participative methods are accepted and used in training.

Objectives

Objective helps the trainer to select the suitable method to deliver the training programme.

Subject Area

Various subject areas have their own specific features as—operations research techniques are based on the use of mathematics and statistics, it is taught through combination of lectures and exercises.

In the programmes such as concentrating on the behavioural aspects of management, the selection should be to analyse the human behaviour. These programmes cause case study methodology, business games, role playing sensitivity training, etc.

Time and Material Factor

Decisions about the choice of teaching methods depend upon time, financial resources and other factors.

Preparation time, affects the cost of teaching material and varies for different teaching material as well. Duration of the course predetermines the kinds of methods to be used. The longer the course, the better are the changes and practical projects.

Methods of Training

Under, on-the-job development a manager serves as a guide for his subordinates. Such a guide or teacher may not be qualified to carry out this important task. He may be lacking skill, interest or patience to educate the subordinates. Therefore, on-the-job development must be properly balanced with classroom (off-the-job) development.

On-the-job Methods

The following are the on-the-job methods:

Coaching

The coaching not only to teach subordinates the necessary skills for doing his assignment but also provide him diversified knowledge so that he may grow and advance.

It makes a manager responsible for teaching apart from his other duties. A manager should recognise his ability to take interest in the training and development of his subordinates.

On-the-job coaching includes learning by doing. The advantage of on the job coaching is that the motivation of the trainee is increased and their problem of learning from theory to practice is minimised.

Understudy

Understudy means to prepare someone to fill the vacancy caused by death, retirement, promotion or transfer of the superior. Also,to get the ideas of his subordinate and give him experience of decision-making and to directly supervise a number of people at work. This gives him an opportunity to try out his leadership skills.

It emphasises learning by doing. It relieves the boss from some of his workload by delegating some portion of his work to the 'understudy'.

Job Rotation

The periodical rotation of executives from one job to another job and from one department to another department on a coordinated and planned basis is a popular means of development among the modern business concerns. The major objective of job rotation is to broaden the background of the executives in the business. It breaks down the feeling of superiority of one department over the other. When a number of executives have served in each other's department, they understand the use of certain function in a particular way. Thus, inter-departmental cooperation enhances.

Special Projects and Committee Assignments

A special project is a training device under which a trainee trainee may be assigned to develop a system of cost control in the execution of an order. The trainee study the problem and then make written recommendations upon it. This project provides valuable experience to the trainee also educate them the importance of costs and to understand the organisational relationships with the accounting department.

Under committee assignments an adhoc committee is constituted and is assigned a subject to discuss and make recommendations. It provides an opportunity to the employee to share in managerial decision making. Committee may be of two types. When committees are an adhoc or temporary nature, sometimes they take on task force activities to ascertain alternate solutions and to make recommendations for implementing a solution.

OFF-THE JOB METHODS

Special Courses

The formal training courses for the executive can be conducted in a number of ways like—

- the organisation may develop the courses itself to be taught to the trainess. And the teaching may be carried out by the instructors from within the organisation and/or by the specialists from other outside institutions.
- sending the personnel to programmes established by colleges and universities.
- the business concern to work with a college or other institution in establishing a course or a series of courses to be taught by its faculty members.

The lecture method is employed in such courses but it is not the only method to depend on. Lectures are also supplemented by group discussions, films, case studies, demonstrations and role plays.

Contents of the Course

Sometimes, the organisation itself designs the courses or where it collaborates with other institutions in this regard, the essential subject-matter covered may include :

Nature and purpose of organisation

Management principles and techniques

Human relations

Technical knowledge and skills.

Economic, social and political environments

The subjects listed above are relevant for all the levels of management. The knowledge and the skill of the executives vary according to the level in which they are involved.

Top management courses emphasise on subjects such as organisation behavior, human relations, financial management etc and manage the overall operations of the organisation and maintain relations both with the insiders and the outsiders.

Role Playing

Role playing techniques is used for human relations and leadership training to give trainees an opportunity to learn human relations skills through practice to evaluate one's own behaviour and its effect on others. Also, itcan be used in human relations training and sales training as well because both these deal with other people.

Under this method, a conflict situation is artificially constructed and two or more trainees are assigned different part to play. The role players are provided either a written or oral description of a situation and the role that they are to play.

Its advantages like–

- to provide an opportunity to develop human relations skills.
- to put into practice the knowledge that they have acquired from text books, lectures, discussions et. It is learning by doing.

Case Study

It provides the trainee an opportunity to apply his knowledge to the solution of realistic problems. As, the trainees apply their knowledge of theory to specific situations. Also, they may be assigned the cases of written analysis and oral class discussion without any prior explanation of concepts and theory.

The success of this method depends upon the qualities of the supervior to conduct the discussion to keep the speakers always on the right track.

Conference Training

It is a training device for the conference member and conference leader. A member learns to respect the viewpoint of others and to develop his skill to motivate people.

This method overcomes certain disadvantages of the lecture, because the participants play active roles. They are not passive. Learning is developed through the implementation of the ideas contributed by the conference member.

Multiple Management

Multiple management gives board members an opportunity to gain knowledge and experience in various aspects of business and to identify those who have good executive talent. Also, the junior executive gain practical experience in group decision-making and in team work. Moreover, it is a less expensive method of development and it permits a considerable number of executives to participate within a reasonable period of time.

Management Games

A management game is a classroom exercise in which teams of students compete against each other to achieve common objective. Under this method, the students learn by analysing the problems and making trial and error type of decisions. A management game provides feed-back on the consequences of business decisions and the feedback is prompt and this facilitates learning.

Syndicate Method

The syndicate method as a technique of teaching meets the requirement of the participants. Syndicate is, a form of organisation for the performance of a specific task of management with the help of a team as much in real life. It helps the participants to use their brain for getting information, rather than get it from other sources. It secures the highest involvement from the participants and it is something like the idea of the 'self –fed groups'.

Sensitivity Training

The sensitivity training are also called Laboratory training, encounter groups, T-Groups, Gestalt therapy, non-verbal groups, self awareness groups, L-group ('L' stand for learning), laboratory education group or group dynamics training.

The goal of sensitivity is helping the trainers to improve quality and participation in human affairs. This method was developed by kurt lewin and later brought into prominence by the National Training Laborities, USA. This method helps leaders and managers to create a more humanistic, people serving system and allow them to see how their behaviour actually affect others. It focuses on exploring the nature of interpersonal relationships.

The duration of programme varies according to specific designs and purpose for which it is used. Most of the groups meet for a total of 10-40 hours. This may be 2 to 6 hours a day in a one or two weeks residential programmes or spread out over several weekends.

Transactional Analysis (TA)

It is an intellectual tool to understand the basis of behaviour and feeling and gives people a rational method for analysing and understanding behaviour when people interact there is social transaction in which one person responds to another. The study of these transactions between people is called Transactional analysis and was developed by Erie Berne for psychotherapy in 1950.

It help us to eradicate or minimise the dysfunctional aspect of our life. The TA programme vary from a day to a five day programme. It involves sharing of concepts and knowledge of TA using structured exercises and game. As in T-Groups, participants examine their personalities, and how they relate to self and others and under preconceived notions, and how they relate to self and others in understanding preconceived notions. It enables the participants to develop interpersonal competence, that, how to improve relationships with self and others so that they change their behaviour appropriately.

INDUCTION TRAINING PRACTICES

Different induction training practices are used in industry such as—

(*i*) Induction guide or check-list are prepared to provide supervisor the information that what induction steps have been taken and what are still to be covered.

(*ii*) The supervisor may take the new workers to work under him and supervise against false impression.

(*iii*) Follow up interview may be taken by the officers of he personnel department permitting the new worker to open up about, supervisor or fellow workers without fear. On the basis of this interview, personnel department can take action to re-assure the workers, gain their confidence and promote their efficiency.

The best method of induction training is talk and pictures. Still, their use depends upon the size of plant, number of new workers to be inducted, etc. Motion picture, visual aids, charts, printed materials etc. are used to explain company policies, processes and products of the company.

TRAINING AIDS

It is a trainer's job to make learning more effective and interesting. The material and the aids selected by the trainer must be suitable to convey the message to the receiver.

The verbal information in written form must be emphasised as a display summary, and it is profitable, before going on to analyse the use of visual aids more deeply.

Non-projected Aids

Without the use of visual aids it is difficult to attract and focus the attention of the trainee, and training is less effective than it may be. It should be remembered, that over 80 per cent of learning takes place through the sense of seeing.

Visual aids are not a substitute for the main techniques of training. Their functions are to illuminate the spoken word. Success in using visual aids depends on the imagination and effort which the trainer gives to the preparation of his material.

The non-projected aids

(*i*) helps the trainee to understand and remember the lectures and other forms of spoken instruction.

(*ii*) provides him added interest and stimulation for learning.

Chalk Board

This consists of board of wood or metal fixed to a wall, on which drawings or writing can be made in chalk. Usually, boards are black in colour, on which white chalk is used. Often dark green and light colored chalks such as yellow are used. The chalkboard is extensively used because materials are easily available and they are very cheap in price.

White Board

It is a smooth plastic finishing, upon which the trainer writes with a felt tip pen. It's effect is more remarkable than black board presentation.

It's advantage is that two types of marker is used over it like alcolhol/spirit based ink and water-based felt tips. Alcohol/spirit based ink is used to draw the outline which is in permanent use. And water based felt tip is used to make visible the additional markings which can be removed by a type of duster. Another advantage of this type of board is that it can also be used as a projection screen when it is cleaned properly.

Magnetic Board

It has steel sheet on which small magnets can be positioned. The board is surfaced with chalk-board paint and the magnetic material is available in strip and sheet form in contrasting colours. It is useful to describe mechanical applications, where movement is most important as there is very little use of diagrams and drawings. Another advantage of this board is quicker and more elaborate presentation of lettering, symbols etc.

Flannel Board or Felt Board

It has a long fibred cloth such as baize, flannel or brushed nylon top with a rough backing to it that can stick. Therefore, it can be used to present the information prepared in advance, particularly charts and diagrams. The board is cheap and easy to make. It is useful to present complex information such as a series of statistics or an organisation chart which can be built up piece by piece.

Plastigraph

It has a smooth plastic surface on which plastic letters, symbols, etc. can be struck. It is similar to flannel board in use but more expensive than a flannel board. If it is intended to re-use the material, care has to be taken in handling and storage.

Flip Charts

It has sheets of paper varying in weight and price. The instructor writes upon the paper with felt-tip pen, crayon, chalk or poster paints. It is a visual aid that has large sales to trainers.

The advantage is that a flip chart is preferable to board work where permanency is required and prepared charts can be stored and used over and over again. It is cheap, clean that covers the previous chart.

Its disadvantages are its size, especially for work involving figures or large diagrams, and the inability to correct mistakes easily. Most flipcharts are extremely portable and look 'modern' as opposed to chalkboard.

Wall Charts

It has sheets of cartridge or similar paper. The charts with good design and presentation are attached to a wall by a variety of methods (tape, plastic, rubber etc.) usually prepared by commercial firms or by the trainer himself. Wall charts can be a great help to the students during the process of memorisation and recall.

Projected Aids

These devices pass light through film or acetate sheeting to project an image on to a suitable screen or mat surface. They have impact when professionally produced film material is used, but could be seen to be 'entertainment' rather than instruction if the trainer do not make full commitment to their use.

Slide Projector

It uses 35mm film and show one frame at a time, controlled by the trainer both for sequence and speed of operation.

The slides can be produced by the trainer or professionally produced.

Tape/slide programmes can be produced in which the slide projector is linked to a tape recorder to give sound commentary either electronically or manually by cueing.

Films

Films of the cinematograph type (usually 35mm) are very common and need no description. As a teaching aid, they must be carefully chosen to explain the core of the lesson.

It's advantage is clearness of the film in displaying the real life like situations.

From the training officer's point of view the film is useful because it can be shown whenever needed and this is an advantage when the same course is being repeated for a series of trainees.

Film-strips

It enables a film to be shown frame-by-frame. It's advantage is in skill training. The major disadvantage is their inability to show movement. But sometimes an actual demonstration is possible by the trainer, or a verbal explanation at the screen, when use a pointer then gets over this difficulty.

Epidiascopes

The epidiascope projects the objects, models, and pages of books, diagrams or slides on the screen.

It requires a constant use of electricity. It is also important that necessary spare parts of the machines should be readily available. It may need the services of an assistant to put the slides or pictures into the machine at suitable points in the lecture. To have good visibility of the image on the screen, the room has to be darkened.

Overhead Projectors

It is a machine that use electricity and projects a picture on the screen. It has two main advantages over the epidiascope.

(*i*) the lecturer can operate the machine himself without turning away from his audience.

(*ii*) do not spend much time to prepare the training materials.

It is popular, portable, reasonably priced and can be used in normal daylight. It helps in maintaining interest, and aids in the organisational aspects of learning, it encourages hierarchical presentation of material because of small surface area. The image of a transparent sheet or plate is projected by a series of mirrors onto a screen.

Audio-visual Aids

It help in the process of learning and education between the trainers and the training group. Some materials which used are—

- Images, pictures, diagrams which are shown by black or white boards, flip charts, printed charts or computer monitors; slide projector etc.
- Motion visuals including films, video-cassettes, filmstrips etc.
- Models or objects for three dimensional presentations.

Through films and videos, the participants can be transferred to a variety of locations over a point, responding to queries of participants and for further reinforcement of learning.

The audio-visual may be used as aids to the lecture or may be used to present an audio or visual case study.

A film can vary the pace of the presentation, provide comic relief, and illustrate concepts as well as provide opportunity for learning from an expert.

Computer with LCD (Liquid Crystal Display)

Computer Based Training (CBT) The computer acts as a tool for the learner and provide calculation, modelling, problem-solving and information facilities.

It involves the use of the computer as a teaching medium and learning resource in an educational or training system.

Television

There are cameras which produce different kinds of pictures in conjunction with a Video Cassette Recorder (VCR). Permanent recordings can be made on video cassettes. However, quite a few trainees feel hesitant to face the camera and are not comfortable with it. Further, this sort of technical facility is costly and due to its being comparatively new, there are not many efficient technical hands available to set it right in case of a fault.

The advantage of CCTV is three-dimensional (3D). The disadvantage is cost and time but it is worth to spend this expenditure. They can be sectionalised to show principles of constructed moving parts of a machine.

MODEL QUESTIONS

1. What is training? Explain objectives and assumptions of training.
2. What are the factors responsible in the selection of a training method?
3. Discuss different methods of training.
4. Focus on teaching aids and their use for the organisations.
5. Write notes on computer with LCD and Television.

Chapter

8 Training Evaluation and ROI

DEFINITION OF TRAINING EVALUATION

It is essential to enhance the effectiveness of training systems. It is a planned process which provides specific information about a selected topic, session, or programme to find out the effectiveness of the programme.

According to Mathis and Jackson: "Evaluation of training compares the post-training results with the objectives expected by administrators, trainers, and trainees."

According to Swierczek and Carmichael: The goals of evaluation are:

- to improve the training programme.
- to provide feedback to programme planners, managers and participation.
- to assess employee skill levels.

OBJECTIVES OF TRAINING EVALUATION

The objectives of training evaluation is to collect data that serve as a valid basis for improving the training system and maintaining quality control over its components. Also the training programmes are designed with prior consideration given to evaluation.

BENEFITS OF TRAINING EVALUATION

The benefits that results from evaluating agency training programmes are:

(*i*) Improved effectiveness and cost effectiveness for training programmes which may result in an increase in resource.

(*ii*) Credibility to the personnelists how to do a better job now or in future programmes.

(*iii*) Commitment and understanding of training by key administrators.

(*iv*) feedback system for developing the strengths and weakness of training participants.

PURPOSES OF TRAINING EVALUATION

According to *Stuffle* and *Beam* the purposes for the evaluation of training programme are:

(*i*) to compare each individual or group with other individual or group.

(*ii*) to compare ideals or standards at different moments.

The purpose of training evaluation affect each step in developing the content and the evaluation components of the training programme.

CRITERIA FOR TRAINING EVALUATION

According to *Suchman,* the personnelist makes use of five general criteria:

(*i*) *Evaluation of effort* assesses input, regardless of output. The questions are addressed "what did you do?" and "how well did you do it"?

(*ii*) *Evaluation of performance* focuses on the results of the programme. This requires clear statements of objectives; it asks "did any change occur?" and "were objectives achieved?"

(*iii*) *Evaluation of adequacy* ensures the effectiveness of the programme. Example, trainees in a programme may show change in practical application, but the number of trainees in the programme may be inappropriate in determining the benefits of the programme.

(*iv*) *Evaluation of efficiency* emphasises on the alternate ways of achieving the goal that are more efficient in terms of time, money, materials, human resources and convenience.

(*v*) *Evaluation of process* focuses on the operation of a training programme that how and why it works or does not work.

Although, some criteria have been tested always but at least four criteria are commonly used in training evaluation– employee reactions to training, learning changes, transfer of training and results.

Employee reactions : Employee reactions are assessed conducting interviews or administering questionnaires to trainess. The Personnelists are interested to know whether trainees liked the programme, whether they thought the instruction was clear and helpful and whether they believe that they learned the material.

Employee learning : The employee are given training material before and after the training to evaluate their learning. Because, personnelists are interested to know how well trainees acquire knowledge, skills, abilities taught in training.

Transfer of training : It examines whether trainees now do things that they could not do before. Has their performance improved? Data which is useful to evaluate transfer of training can be obtained through interviews of trainees and observation of job performance.

Results : Results are evaluated by measuring the effect of training on the achievement of agency objectives.

Process of the Training Evaluation

To evaluate a training programme the process starts after setting the evaluation criterion, based on the objectives of the programme. The knowledge or skill level of the training is also tested before the programme.

Pre-training Evaluation: This is prior to the course. The existing level of knowledge and skills are reassessed. This is carried out through a series of questionnaires, discussions and workshops. Once such evaluation is carried out, the appropriateness of the context and design are established.

Input and Delivery Evaluation: The course inputs are done either individually or through group evaluation methods. Many management development programmes have schedules for simultaneous review. Each topic of the module is evaluated in terms of its content, presen-tation, relevance and applicability/usefulness.

The last day of the course a questionnaire is given to the participants to assess improvement in skills comparing with pre training data. Moreover, to collect general information about the course inputs and the impressions about the course.

Post Training Evaluation: To enhance individual effectiveness and improvement in organisational performance improvement plans are prepared and implemented on time bound basis approved by the trainers and superiors in the organisation.

After a lapse of 6-12 months the results obtained are used to evaluate the applicability of training. The assessment of organisation improvements is examined and the contributions of trainees towards new introduction like quality circles, suggestions schemes, ISO 9000, TQM process are seen as individual trainee's contributions.

The results of this test are compared with the results of a post-training test to assess the learning from the training programme. The learning of the workers and the transfer of knowledge to the job decides the success of training imparted. After a few months, follow-up studies help in assessing the retention and application of the knowledge gained in training.

APPROACHES TO TRAINING EVALUATION

The effort in the training evaluation is made without any specific model but concentrates to justify the expenditure at a success-cum-achievement aspect. So, the results are codified in a language that suits to the taxpayers, decision-makers and others, who are told that a given training programme 'did what it promised to do'. Sometimes, the classical and contemporary evaluation models fall in this category.

The Classical Evaluation Model

It assumes that the goals and objectives of training can be identified and translated into measureable standards; so there is no need for experimental and control studies for comparisons.

The Contemporary Evaluation Model

These models provides data for policy formulation, decision-making and define the goals and objectives of training at the project planning stage.

The Goal Attainment Model

It can be done involving the evaluator right from the stage of planning of projects till fixing training objectives under a given time-frame. It is based on the assumptions that if the goals and objectives are seperated at different stages then fixing-up of criteria or standard and use of proper evaluation methodologies can be ensured.

The System Model

It identifies the sub-systems and individuals, groups and community which are capable to achieve and observe the training goals.

The system model has two main drawbacks; (*i*) there is difficulty in changing the objectives of training in a sub-system and in probing analysis; and (*ii*) the programme of training is a software production which allows outside influences which is not pure because it is contaminated by external influences (including biases of evaluators also).

CIRO Framework

One of the most common ways of training evaluation is named 'CIRO Framework' of evaluation. CIRO stands for Context, Input, Reaction and Outcome.

Context Evaluation: Obtaining and using information about the individual and organisational problems. It indicates the assessment of training needs as a basis for decision.

Input Evaluation: Obtaining and using information about the training resources in order to choose alternative inputs to training.

Reaction Evaluation: Obtaining and using information about the trainees on evaluation and reactions, in order to improve training. This framework is based on three simple and fundamental questions, which the trainer must constantly ask. These questions are as follows:

(*i*) What needs to be changed?

(*ii*) What procedures are most liked to bring about this change?

(*iii*) What evidence is there that change has occurred?

The first two question must be settled before any training begins. The third question, can be answered after the training has been completed.

Outcome Evaluation: Monitoring the consequences of training. Three levels of outcome evaluation may be distinguished as follows:

(*i*) *Immediate Outcomes:* The changes in trainees' knowledge, skill and attitudes can be identified after the completion of training. The assessment is usually done in terms of changed behaviour during a training programme.

(ii) Intermediate Outcomes: The changes in trainees' actual work behavior results after training. The assessment is usually done in terms of performance on the job and long-term outcomes.

(iii) Ultimate Outcomes: The changes in the functioning of organisation results from changes in work behaviour. The assessment is usually in terms of output or financial measures.

Kirkpatrick's Model

One more popular framework for training evaluation is known as 'Kirkpatrick's Model'. which has four steps as:

(i) Reaction: How well did the trainees like the programme?

(ii) Learning: What principles, facts and techniques were learned?

(iii) Behaviour: What changes in job behavior resulted?

(iv) Results: What were the tangible results?

Reaction Stage: This is evaluated based on the objectives set at three levels. It is important that training objectives are carefully thought and framed.

(i) Ultimate Objectives: The particular defect in the organisation that he is hoping to remove.

(ii) Intermediate Objectives: The changes in employees work behaviour is necessary if the ultimate objective is to be attained.

(iii) Immediate Objectives: The new knowledge, skills or attitudes employees must acquire before they change their behaviour in the required way.

Learning Stage: The information of learning is evaluated irrespective of whether the trainees apply the learning on the job or not. Learning can be in the areas of knowledge, skill or attitude.

Semantic Differential Scales (SDS)

This is the simplest and effective form of evaluation. The trainees are given a sheet, at the top of which the subject matter of training is stated (for example, 'cost reduction') and below this, number of seven point or five point scales stretching between pairs of adjectives with opposite meanings. (For example, 'inefficient-efficient'; 'complicated-simple'; 'friendly-hostile' and so on). They are asked to rate the subject matter of training at the beginning and at the end of training so that changes can be identified.

Job Behaviour Change

At this stage change in behaviour is evaluated. The trainer involves himself with the trainee on the job so that guidance, if required, could be given. The other approach is to motivate the line manager to control the trainee to become a facilitator of this transfer.

FAILURE OF TRAINING EVALUATION

Often, it is observed that the training programme evaluations fails due to inadequate planning or designing, lack of objective evaluation, errors of one sort or another, improper interpretation of result and inappropriate use of results. Some of these mistakes can be easily overcome through planning, while some are difficult.

Inadequate Planning

To make a training programme evaluation effective it must be planned carefully. There are some common deficiencies in planning which are—

- failure to make clear all the concerned purposes of the evaluation.
- failure to follow specific procedures and to work out the details of the programme, scheduling of surveys, interviews and observations.

- failure to train trainers the principles and techniques of evaluation for the use of data gathering instruments.

Lack of Objectivity

It is not possible to say that training programme evaluation is completely objective, there are some steps that can be considered to make objective clear and better—

- train the trainers
- design appropriate data-gathering instruments
- look at all the components of the training situation as an integrated system

Rater's Errors

The difference of the observers to evaluate the quality of performance or materials in their rating. There are some errors that occur by faults in the design of rating instruments, some occur by certain groups of observers, and some by individual observers. It is observed that there are some typical categories of rating error : central tendency, halo effect and recency.

Improper Interpretation of Data

The meaning and impact of the data are judged properly, otherwise, the value of the information collected will be completely lost. Here, are some of the mistakes in the interpretation of data from training programmes.

(*i*) to assume that an observation or judgment made by only one observer or group of trainees is inaccurate or invalid.

(*ii*) to accept comments or responses of unlimited questions in general and not considering the problems of language and it's meanings.

(*iii*) to fail to consider the aims and objectives of the individuals providing the data.

Inappropriate Use of Evaluation Results

Sometimes, the results of evaluation are not used for the exact purposes which are as follows:

(*i*) Using data and reports on a single part of a training programme to make decisions on the whole programme.

(*ii*) Using data and reports on the whole training programme to make decisions for future training programs.

(*iii*) Using unsupported and invalidated data as a basis for making significant changes to a training programme or system.

RETURN ON INVESMENT (ROI)

To spend money on faith is decreasing in the organisation and the pressure is increasing to justify T&D expenses. So now, it is necessary for those in the field *to focus* on the evaluation of T&D and to properly show and communicate to the top management that T&D efforts are making worthwhile contributions for the betterment of the organisation.

Without training new technology cannot be acquired and implemented successfully. The profit gained by giving proper training and the losses incurred due to inadequate training are too high, which cannot be ignored. The net value of training increases with it's expansion throughout the organisation.

There are many examples where organisation have no idea whether there is any change in employees' approach after attending the training programmes. A marketing services company organised an extensive sales training programme, but when asked after six months that whether anyone was using the new presentation skills, management had no idea. They New that training programme was not successful as no one could purchase the new product/service.

So, the question is 'Is it fair on the part of any organisation to come *to such conclusion* without doing any evaluation exercise'? But, in practice when management find training as unsuccessful, then it is considered that training is an additional expense that needs to be cut whenever possible. But, when it is conducted appropriately it results in significant Return on Investment.

Process of Calculating ROI

To calculate Return on Investment, trainer must first make the estimates of the costs and benefits associated with a training programme. The calculate ROI, it consists of two major parts namely, costs of design and development and forecasting and measuring.

Costs of Design and Development

The first category of cost is the design and development of the training programme, whether this comprises of classroom events, self-study materials, simple coaching sessions or some combination. It considers—

(*i*) Costs of external designers and developers.

(*ii*) Cost of design and development (purchase of copyrights, travel, expenses, etc.)

Promotional Costs: To promote the training programmes the organisations make effort. This category of costs is promotional costs that considers—

(*i*) The internal days of promotional activity.

(*ii*) The costs of external agencies.

(*iii*) The costs of promotion (posters, brochures, etc.)

Administration Costs: This is an another category of costs. An allowance is given for the spent time by the training department in administrating the training programme. This is a factor for the number of students. It considers—

(*i*) Hours of administration required per student.

(*ii*) Direct administration costs per student (joining materials, registration fees, etc.)

Faculty Costs: The another category of costs is the delivery of training, whether this is conducted by faculty (tutors, instructors, coaches, etc.) or is self-administered (workbooks, CBT, online training etc.). The informations that needed to calculate faculty costs are—

(*i*) The number of students going through the programme.

(*ii*) Hours of group training (whether classroom-based or delivered in real time, online).

(*iii*) Hours of one-to-one training (typically face-to-face, by telephone, video conferencing link or in real-time, online).

(*iv*) Hours of self-study training.

(*v*) Additional faculty hours (preparation time, the time needed to review or mark given work or the time needed to correspond by email or bulletin boards with online students).

(*vi*) Faculty expenses (travel, accommodation, sustenance, etc.)

Material Costs: There are cost of materials also which are as follows:

(*i*) Cost per student of training materials (books, manuals, consumables, etc.)

(*ii*) Licence cost per student for use apart from things needed for study.

Facilities Costs: The trainers are also the cost of the training facilities. These includes the rental or assumed internal cost of the following:

(*i*) Training rooms.

(*ii*) Open learning/self-study rooms.

(*iii*) Equipment used.

Student Costs: It is also one of the most significant delivery cost. So, it is necessary to charge a student's cost against the programme, if training is undertaken in time. So the trainer only need to estimate the amount of travel and training that is undertaken in productive work time not in slack time, breaks or outside the work hours.

When an employee attend a training programme during the work time, the organisation does not only pays that person's payroll costs, rather it also loose the opportunity for that person to add value to the organisation.

Forecasting and Measuring Benefits

The major categories of benefits are as follows :

Labour Savings: Labour saving is realised if the labour applied to a job is reduced, whether this comes as a result of redundancies, transfers of staff to new positions or re-allocation of work. If the time saving result in slow down of work, then there is no saving example—

Reduced effort, less time spent correcting the mistakes, faster access to information.

Productivity Increases: Productivity increases as a result of training.Example, improved methodologies reducing the effort required,higher levels of skill leading faster work, higher levels of motivation leading to increased effort.

Other Cost Savings: Cost saving is achieved in many ways, not only through the savings in labor but also allowing the trainer to make assessment of the following like-machine breakdowns, lower staff turnover, training costs, a reduction in bad debts.

Other Income Generation: It is possible for new income to be generated in some job as a direct result of training. Sometimes, this can be recorded as a productivity increase, but at times when a direct and specific analysis is required.

Calculating ROI: The return on investment indicates the percentage of return the trainer has made over a specified period investing in a training programme. The trainer likes to specify a period that fits well with the organisation's planning cycle—may be a year or two years. On the other hand, he may wish to calculate the period of benefit of an average trainee in which they apply the knowledge and skills being taught.

The formula used for calculating ROI is :

% ROI = (benefits/costs) × 100

Payback Period: The months taken before the benefits of training match the costs and the training pays for itself is called as a payback period of a training programme, which can be calculated as follows:

Payback period = costs/monthly benefits

Payback period is a powerful measure. If the figure is relatively low—perhaps only a few months—then management is more encouraged to make the training investment. As a measure, there is an advantage that it does not require any arbitrary benefit period to be specified.

CRITERIA FOR MEASURING TRAINING SUCCESS

To measure success in training programme the following are some elements to be considered like—

Numbers: It is a way to measure the success of training is the presence of the number of participants during the training', Although, it is not a true measure of the effectiveness of training, increased number of participants do indicate that the training is quite successful and the design and methodology is up to the mark.

Direct Cost: The costs that are incurred directly as a result of training program like external design and development, consultancy fees, travel expenses and so on is direct costs. If the programme do not take place, these costs are not incurred. Some of the organisation only take direct costs into consideration to measure the training costs.

Indirect Cost: This cost is not directly associated with a training event, but incurs anyway, whether or not training took place. Any analysis of the costs of training includes both direct and indirect costs.

Efficiency: It is a measure of the amount of learning achieved in comparison to the amount of effort put in. Practically, it means the amount of time it takes to complete a piece of training.

Performance to Schedule: Sometimes for a training programme, time is a critical factor so it needs to be completed within a given date if a particular business objective is to be achieved.

Income Received: The income received is a vital measure of its success, If the training provider operates externally to a client organisation.

The Extent to Which Trainees Mix: Group event, provides an opportunity for trainees to work in different departments or regions to meet with each other, share experiences and make contacts. Because, this is a profitable outcome of training, it needs to be considered to compare training methods.

Reactions: If trainees react negatively to the training programmes they are less expected to transfer their knowledge what they learnt in their work and more likely to give bad reports to their juniors due to which number of students decrease.

Learning: It can be measured with the help of a test or exam or some form of assessed exercise. If a student has to achieve a certain level of learning to obtain a 'pass mark', then the pass outs is used as an evaluation measure. Another important aspect of learning is the degree of retention that is how much of the learning has been retained by a trainee after the course is over.

Behaviour Change: To assess behavior change it requires that the measurements must be taken before and after the training.

Performance Change: With the help of different methods the impact of training performance is measured like numbers of complaints, sales made, output per hour and so on.

MODEL QUESTIONS

1. Discuss training evaluation and its benefits.
2. Discuss purpose of training evaluation.
3. Give focus on the approaches to training evaluation.
4. What is ROI?
5. What are the criteria to measure training success?

Chapter

9 Trainer and Training Styles

A training officer must be aware of possible training courses, and the subjects and techniques suitable for everyone. He needs to have a thorough knowledge of the activities of his organisation and are expected to advise on training requirements whether for existing activities or new activities of the organisation.

The most successful training officer is one who makes managers interested in training so that they come to him and tell him what training they want. At the same time, the training officer must admit to the fact that if a training course or programme leads to improved job performance the credit goes to the supervisor.

ROLES OF TRAINER

According to Benett, there are five key roles of a trainer as—

- The trainer
- The provider
- The consultant
- The innovator
- The manager

The trainer and provider role is to maintain performance. Whereas, the consultant and innovator role is to bring change. And the last one, the manager is concerned with to integrate the activities and behaviours.

These roles are not distinct packages of activities, behaviours and responsibilities. Each have a clear focus and relate to each other, as mentioned earlier.

The Trainer

The trainer's role is to help people to learn and provide feedback about their learning and adopt course designs to meet trainees' needs. The trainer's role involve classroom teaching, laboratory work, small group work, supervision of individual project work and other activities that influence immediate learning experiences.

The Provider

The provider of the training programme makes analysis for training needs; setting objectives; designing courses; choosing suitable methods; and evaluating courses or training activities and helping trainers to deliver the training.

The Consultant

The responsibility is to work with providers and trainers to establish training programmes, advise training managers and possible training solutions on training goals and policies.

The Innovator

They are concerned to provide support and help to managers to cope with change; identify where seminars and workshops can be a useful means to educate managers for change; facilitate change to identify the real sources of power in the organisation etc.

The Manager

The main role of manager is to set training goals, policies and plans, liaison with other departments; ensure that suitable training activities are designed, developed, delivered and evaluated; establish effective line of authority and communicate within the training department; monitor quality standards and control the activities against a total training plan.

PERSONALITY OF TRAINER

There are some constituents that reflect the differences between the effective and ineffective trainers.

Teaching Effectiveness

It is a multiple function of a number of factors, *e.g.*, intelligence, interpersonal warmth, social insight, shrewdness, imaginativeness, ego-strength, lack of tension etc.

Leadership Style

The leadership style coordinates the group activities, sets the tone of interactions and establish goals and tasks for the group. As a group leader his ideas and suggestions are considered important.

Interpersonal Competence

It's important aspect is the ability of the person to perceive and remain prompt in his judgment, and emphatic to social obligations and reactions of others.

Psychological Needs

A trainer who has a high need for achievement falls in the category of effective group discussion leaders and differs from the ineffective leaders. The need to nurture and care appears to be another need of trainer which produces long-term positive changes in the group's behaviour and attitudes.

Ego Strength

Egoistic people are well suited for flexible jobs and they can make adjustments with external difficulties and interpersonal conflicts and can deal with new and ambiguous situations.

BEHAVIOUR OF TRAINER

The participant's skill of innovation, independent working and collaboration fully depends upon the approach and behaviour of trainers specially—when the task is clear and attractive to the participants and when the task is clear but unattractive to the participants.

When the Task is not Clear to Participants

When participants do not know what to do or how to proceed the problem at the time trainers help them.

On the other hand, trainers can also understand themselves as:

- Participants are confused.
- Guess for the cause of their confusion.
- With the help of diagnosis provide feedback and support and guide them.
- Expect that the participants can now understand the task.

If, anything is not clear among participants' then trainers quickly clarify it.

When the task is Clear and Attractive to the Participants

The trainers help participants to broaden their issue, challenge their understanding, help them to evaluate ends and means and get the advantage out of a particular task and their collaboration. When the task is clear and attractive, the effects of direct and indirect influence are different from the effects of the task which is questionable or unattractive.

When the Task is Clear but Unattractive to the Participants

When the task is clear but unattractive to the participants then it means that participants do not want to do it. So, trainers use their authority to make them do the task either by rewarding or punishing them. In many ways, trainers help participants to reassess their goals and make new plans. When trainers use indirect influence; the indicators show different results and sudden interaction among participants; without knowing who will take what role next.

UNCLARITY OF TRAINER

The trainer who feels pressures everyday as a challenge to his authority in the programme and institution deals with them differently from a trainer who sees them arising out of the participants' efforts. There are three confusions that generally arise for a trainer-Participants expectations *vs.* Trainers intentions, Individual *vs.* Group needs and Consistency vs. Flexibility.

Participant's Expectations *vs.* Trainer's Intentions

Participants have expectations with the trainers when they first meet. The expect to learn new things which they do not know. Trainers ask question with the new group. Their intention may be to ascertain how well the group members have understood the concepts in the training program. With experience trainers have realized that some participants hesitate to ask due to fear of being ridiculed and some ask questions to show their worth.

Individuals *vs.* Group Needs

Most of the participants differ in interests, working style, learning capacity and their interpretation of a trainer's behaviour. But, except for minor modifications the trainer's actions have to be the same for all. To pay attention on people at extremes is easiest and often difficult to avoid example, quick or slow talkers or silent etc.

Consistency *vs.* Flexibility

Participants expects trainers to be consistent, faultless and successful. They know how to deal with trainers and what to expect from them from the day one.

Trainers express this freedom at the personal level properly what according to Carl Rovers is their reality and interdependence responding to others.

Effective trainers are congruent, authentic, real and is based on discussions and on statistical correlations between predicted and actual ratings.

ATTRIBUTES OF TRAINING PROGRAMME

The attributes of training programme are the trainer, the trainees, the curriculum, the training materials, the time and sequencing, location, physical facilitates and training equipments.

The Trainer

A good trainer must have general, technical and specialised knowledge of the subject. His experience and skills reflect in handling the working sessions, adapting his training style and techniques. Also, generating interest in characteristics and attitudes like-openness to new ideas, observation powers, questioning mind and willingness to experiment.

The Trainees

The trainees must have necessary background, experience, intellectual and physical capacities and care to avoid disparity in the group. The trainee must form a homogenous group with respect to their past experiences, knowledge and potential for learning,.

The Curriculum (Course of Study)

The curriculum should be designed for the best utilisation of resources available. The importance of curriculum must be ensured to the trainee in respect of its degree of complexity on the job to be performed by him.

The Training Material

The training material must be according to the need and the media of presentation to the subject under consideration. Articles or pamphlets for a particular topic should be suitably indexed to avoid duplication of effort.

The Methods and Techniques

The training method and techniques must be attractive for the participants to induce a transfer of knowledge and skills.

The Timing and Sequencing

The timing and sequencing of sessions must be done depending upon the quantity of material to cover, the availability of trainers and trainees and the content of the programme.

Location

The training venue should be equipped with freedom, ventilation, peace and overall facilities whenever needed. For large classes, a U-shaped seating arrangement with the instructor at the lowest elevation is advisable.

The Physical Facilities and Training Equipment

The availability of certain basic facilities like overhead projector, should be ensured.

CHALLENGES BEFORE TRAINERS

As, the profile of workers has changed due to fast changes in our system so the profile of managers has also changed. One major source of new managers is the management institutions. Some of the institutions have adopted case study method developed by Harvard Business School- the premier management institution in the world. Others concentrate on their quantitative methods like—

Set Goals—Establish Policies and Procedures

- Implement change
- Get results and produce respectable growth
- Profitability and return on investment

According to Michael Silva and Craig Hickman the new age skills are :

- Creative insight
- Sensitivity
- Vision
- Versatility
- Focus
- Patience

Change in Attitude

The test of success of training can be carried out finding the change in the attitude to practice or implement the knowledge and skills. For testing the 'change in attitude', post-course evaluations can be carried out, seminars can be held, time to time in which previous participants feedback can be obtained.

Our nation can be elevated through the training and retraining of personnel which is one of the most effective tools. This tool can be effective only when various factors, are kept in view and practiced by trainers honestly and sincerely. A successful training not only makes the person competent to perform his job efficiently but also prepares him to shoulder higher responsibilities. This improves the process of presentation also. A successful training programme widens the overall horizon of the trainee and generates understanding of various problems and view points of others

TRAINER'S STYLE

The task of the trainer is to develop their own style that suits them and they find effective. The behaviours of trainers confirm some useful points as—

- to develop self awareness in them
- others aim to bring new knowledge to bear on practical problems, and
- to heighten the participants urge to study further to lifelong learning.

They pay attention to participants, training content and to the process itself. In fact, some of them express their opinions while some do not express their opinion, some address the participants as a group and others little. And no one assures good results or bad ones.

They are flexible when they interact with participants. They show specific behaviour to situational needs. This is like contingency management in training. Experienced trainers choose suitable situation in the session as well as differing needs. In the terminology of transactional analysis, an effective trainer may have all age states—parent, adult and child which help participants to mature and become able to cope with their lives and circumstances.

Role of New Technology in Training Styles

Some technology is well established while some is only at the environment stage and not clear in the field of management development.

Technology for distance learning creates and delivers materials which facilitate learning. The use of open and distance learning in the management field is already being carried out by a number of forces.

What will happen later on is uncertain, one of the key factors is the educational quality of programmes or packages which becomes available.

NEW OPPORTUNITIES IN TRAINING

The role of technology modifies the methodology of training programme for the convenience of the participants to undergo training programme. There is a one important method like, distance learning which is explained below.

Distance Learning

The distance learning programme is used to train a large number of participants with the introduction of new technologies. It's advantage is to keep people on the job and make them learn at their own pace and simplify the requirements of different organisations to collaborate in training.

Distance learning of all kinds combines the training needs of a large group and prepare relevant curricula for meeting their needs. Then select a suitable media mix, prepare a series of modules to be used by individual or small group of participants, review the progress of participants and give feedback to them on what they have been able to learn well and where they need to improve further.

Advantages of Distance Learning

The advantages of distance learning method are discussed below:

(*i*) It overcomes some of the traditional barriers of training like—location, inflexible schedules, cost and style and includes specifically designed materials.

(*ii*) All course elements are completely integrated.

(*iii*) There are no present starting and finishing dates imposed from outside. Programs can be studied as and when suitable to the individual or to the organisation.

(*iv*) It provides an opportunity to increase the productivity of the training function providing high quality reliable materials that can reach to a large audience

(*v*) Where one or two managers need training in a particular skill, the programmes can be used individually with regular tutorials and reviews.

(*vi*) Where large numbers require training in a particular location, in-Company group exercises and discussions can be incorporated with the basic material.

MODEL QUESTIONS

1. Discuss the roles and personality of trainer.
2. Explain behaviour of the trainer and how it is useful for the participants.
3. What are the dilemmas or confusion for the trainers?
4. Give focus on the challenges of the trainers.
5. Describe trainers style for training.

Chapter

10 Performance Appraisal

CONCEPT

The performance of an organisation is managed monitoring the performance of the individual employees in the organisation. So, the successful performance of an organisation is a culmination of individual performances and contributions.

Performance appraisal can be defined as the process of evaluating the performance of an employee and communicating the results of evaluation to him for the purpose of rewarding or developing the employee.

The term performance appraisal is concerned with the process of rating an employee's worth to an organisation, with a view to increase it. So, most of the performance appraisal systems are linked to rewards systems as well as employee development systems. It is also important that the appraisal system matches the organisational culture. For example, a 360 degree feedback systems, would not deliver results if it is implemented in a traditional organisation which has rigid hierarchies.

Although, performance appraisal and potential evaluation are used synonymously, but performance appraisal is a wider term than potential evaluation. The potential evaluation evaluates the different traits of the employee by comparing the qualitative factors such as nature of the individual, physical and mental ability etc. Whereas performance appraisal evaluates the performance of an employee by comparing the quantitative factors such as quantity of output and rejected output, standard of work etc.

According to Flippo *"Performance appraisal is a systematic, periodic and so far as humanly possible and impartial rating of an employee's excellence in matters pertaining to his present job and to his potentialities for a better job".*

Whereas,

According to Flippo *"Potential evaluation attempts to systematic, periodic and so far as humanly possible, an impartial rating of an employee's excellence in matters pertaining to his present job and to his potentialities for a job."*

PURPOSES OF PERFORMANCE APPRAISAL

- to improve job performance and identify the potentialities for other work.
- To identify the need and areas for further training of the employees.
- To assist in determining promotion and transfer policies.
- To reduce the grievances among the employees
- To make the compensation plans more scientific and rational.
- To help in proper placement of the workers after the completion of their training.
- To facilitate research in personnel management.
- To develop positive relations in between superior and subordinate.

Q. What is appraisal and how it is to be implemented ?

- It is a two way discussion between the appraiser and the appraisee.

- It is a pen document that both appraiser and the appraisee agrees and sign.
- It is a plan for future.
- It is a constructive criticism of the performance and personality of the appraisee in the immediate past.
- It's meeting without emotions are being involved.

THE APPRAISAL PROCESS

1. The first step in the appraisal process is to find out the standards of performance based on the organisation objectives and the job description. It is easier to evaluate performance, if goals and standards are specific and quantifiable.
2. The second step in the appraisal process is the measurement of employee performance against pre-determined goals and standards.
3. The third step is the actual process of measurement. Performance appraisal is a continuous process and the feedback should be given to the employee at regular intervals. This helps the employees to track their performance and grooms them for higher responsibilities.
4. The fourth step is communicating the results of appraisal to the employee concerned. It is the responsibility of the manager to make the employee feel comfortable with the whole process.
5. The final step is to put into effective use. Whatever may be the organisational policy, *the document* of appraisal has to be put into use effectively and immediately to ensure a better performance during the next appraisal period.

Many organisations do not get acceptance and support from their employees for their performance appraisal system because of lack of commitment of the top management.

Limitations

Performance appraisal may not yield the desired results because of the following deficiencies :

- if the factors included in the assessment are irrelevant, the result of potential evaluation is not accurate.
- different qualities to be evaluated may not be given proper weightage in certain cases.
- some of the factors are highly subjective like initiative and personality of the employees so that actual evaluation may not be on scientific lines.
- supervisor often do not have critical ability in assessing the staff. Sometimes, they are guided by their personal emotions and likes. So, the evaluation are likely to be biased.

Effective Appraisal System

An appraisal system to be effective it needs to be based on the following elements :

- the performance appraisal should be performance based, uniform and non variable, fair, just and equitable. It should be ensured that the appraisers are honest, rational and objective in their approach, judgement and behavioral operation.
- Periodic goal setting
- Periodic or annual assessment of performance in terms of such goals –
  (*a*) identifying facilitating and inhabitating factors in relation to the achievement of goals.
  (*b*) Development of action plans for overcoming inhabitating factors and strengthening the facilitating factors.
- the results of performance appraisal must be immediately communicated to the employees

especially when they are negative so that they may try to improve their performance and also they may be able to know where do they stand.

- Periodic review of behaviour which contributes to management effectiveness.
- Identification of development needs

THE APPRAISERS

The employee in coordination with his supervisor, decides the performance objectives and standards. After the appraisal period the appraiser offers his opinion to the employee. Then employee on the basis of the opinion of appraiser assesses his own performance, in comparison to the pre-determined objective.

In 360 degree feedback system, the peers of the employee, suppliers, customers and even his subordinates helps in the identification of problem areas.

Self-Appraisal

The employee on the basis of his strength and weaknesses evaluates his performance and easily identifies the problem areas that need training and development.

Supervisors

The supervisor has a very important role in the appraisal of his subordinates. Many of them fear to take the exercise, as they do not want to spoil their relationship with the employee.

Peers

Peer appraisal is used to assess the communication and interpersonal skills of the employee, which can affect the team performance.

Customer/Clients

In service organisation like banks and hotels, customer feedback is most important tool in evaluating performance of the employee. In manufacturing organisation, the internal customer evaluates the performance of the employee.

Subordinates

The subordinate evaluates the performance of his supervisor which is prevailing fast in most of the organisations. Example, in 360 degree feedback system, the appraisal by subordinates is being adopted by many organisations.

PERFORMANCE APPRAISAL METHODS

The different appraisal methods used by the organisations are :

Traditional Methods

1. Management by Objectives or goal-setting
2. Graphic rating scale
3. Work standards approach
4. Essay appraisal
5. Critical incident method
6. Forced choice rating method
7. Point allocation method
8. Ranking methods
9. Checklist

Modern Methods

1. Behaviourally anchored rating scale (BARS)
2. 360 degree performance appraisal
3. Team appraisals
4. Balanced scorecard method

Management by Objectives (MBO)

Management by objectives is also called goal-setting approach. It is more commonly used for managers and professionals. For successful implementation of MBO, the following are required:

- measurable goals
- suitable and motivated employees
- regular feedback
- evaluation of performance and corrective action

Graphic Rating Method

This method rates the employee on factors like quantity and quality of work, job knowledge, dependability, punctuality, attendance etc. Graphic rating scale includes numerical ranges as well as written descriptions.

There are two disadvantages of this method. One disadvantage is that the important ones may get missed out and the irrelevant ones may get included. The second disadvantage is that different people may interpret the written descriptions in different ways.

Work Standards Approach

This method of appraisal is suitable in a manufacturing scenario, where the goals are pre-determined work standard. The advantage of this approach is that the goals are measurable. The disadvantage is that the work standards for different job categories cannot be compared.

Essay Appraisal

In the Essay Appraisal method, questions or guidelines are provided to the appraiser, based on that he analyses and describes the employee's performance. If the appraiser concentrates on a single aspect or misses out an important aspect of performance the appraisal will be incomplete or inadequate. Similarly, it is difficult to compare the performance of two employees, based on the descriptions of their performance provided by different supervisors. The advantage of this system is that the appraiser can express his views on the employee's performance, without any constraints.

Critical Incident Method

In this method the appraiser makes a record of all the critical incidents that reflect the performance or behavior of the employee during the appraisal period. At the end of the appraisal period, this record forms the basis for the evaluation of performance of the employee. This method of appraisal is rarely used because of the ambiguity involved and the effort required in recording the incidents.

Forced Choice Rating Method

In this method, the appraiser assign ranks to different attributes of the employee. Once, the employee attributes are ranked, the human resource department applies weights and arrives at a score which is the final appraisal score.

Point Allocation Method

In this method of appraisal, the appraiser assigns different points to different members in his team based on their performance during the appraisal period. The best performer gets the highest score and the last one in the team gets the least score. One disadvantage is that an appraiser can allocate equal points to everyone in the group, ignoring the differences in their performance. Another disadvantage is that the difference in point allocation may not reflect the differences in performances across groups.

Ranking Methods

There are three commonly used methods of ranking- as alternation, paired comparison and forced distribution. The first two methods are used when there are only a few employees to be ranked, whereas forced distribution method is used in large companies like GE, Microsoft and Wipro, where thousands of employees are to be ranked.

In the first method, alternation, the appraiser ranks all his employees based on their performance and contributions to the organisation. In the paired comparison method, the appraiser ranks the employees, based on paired comparison. The forced distribution method is very popular method of performance appraisal in big organisations. In this method the employees are categorised as 'Top', 'Standard' and 'Bottom' and placed under a forced-distribution.

Checklist

In this method, weights are attached to each of the questions based on which the final appraisal score of the employee is calculated. Major disadvantage is that different checklist is designed for different jobs that may make the whole exercise cumbersome and complex.

Behaviourally Anchored Rating Scale (BARS)

BARS concentrates on the behavioural traits instead of his actual performance.

There are three steps in implementing BARS system. They are:

1. Determination of different job aspects by the manager and the employee.
2. Determination of the parameters to be used and grouping of traits for each scale parameters, based on consensus.
3. Identification of different traits by the manager and the employee for each job dimension.

The main advantage of BARS is that both the manager and the employees are actively involved in the appraisal process. One drawback of this system is it is inconvenient and takes much time in development.

360 Degree Performance Appraisal

In this ystem, the employee's performance is evaluated by the peers, customers, suppliers and subordinates of the employee, who are directly affected by his behaviour and performance, apart from the boss. It is held annually and conducted in the following ways.

- Self appraisal
- Subordinate
- HOD's/Functional Head
- Outside agencies like customers, venders, dealers, govt agencies.
- By the superiors, while giving ratings all the above 3 & 4 levels of rating must be submitted to him before he gives his own ratings
- Appraisal committee represented by Sr. Managers.

Team Appraisals

In the team appraisal method, the individual team members evaluate their colleagues in the team and provide feedback. This helps in coordinating individual efforts and taking the group performance to higher levels.

Balanced Scorecard

This method while measuring performance concentrates the efforts of people to achieve organisational goals. The assigning of responsibilities to individuals and tracking for achievement of objectives is called HR scorecard. The HR scorecard seeks to give online feedback to the employees as to how they are faring. In some cases, their salaries are linked to their performance. It is a part of balanced scorecard.

Many top Indian companies like Infosys, i2 Technologies, Godrej Consumer Products, GTL, ITC Ltd. and Mahindra & Mahindra are using this method of performance management.

THE APPRAISAL INTERVIEW

In modern organisations the employee himself evaluates his own performance on various factors mentioned in the appraisal form and assesses his strengths and weaknesses. This helps him to identify the areas that need training or development inputs.

Challenges of Appraisal Interview

The atmosphere in an appraisal interview is usually comfortable, as the appraisee is apprehensive in receiving any negative feedback and the appraiser is cautios of giving such feedback. So, Some of the main challenges of an appraisal interview are:

The Organisation Culture: If, there is absence of right kind of organizational culture then it leads to an ineffective process of performance appraisal.

Boss-employee Relationship: The general relationship between the employee and his boss is the biggest factor of the interview.

The Maturity Level of the Individuals: If the supervisor gives a feedback saying that the employee needs to improve in a few areas, an immature or unprofessional individual may react in a defensive way, leading to unpleasantness.

A Cautious Appraiser: The appraiser, with a view to maintain a cordial relationship with appraise, may restrain to give any negative or constructive feedback. This makes the whole exercise futile.

A Partial Appraiser: Often, the appraiser may be partial or against the appraisee for various reasons. This may lead to negative feedback, which renders the exercise futile.

Lack of Experience: Lack of experience to the process of performance appraisal may result ineffective which may not benefit the individual or the organization.

DRAWBACKS IN PERFORMANCE APPRAISAL

Some of the constituents that affect the appraisal process at an individual level are:

Culture : The culture of the organization or the country influence the appraiser to rate the appraise in a particular way.

Stereotyping : It involves judging someone based on the group he belongs to and the appraiser's perception of the group. For example - An appraiser who believes that women may be good managers so rate his female appraisees better than his male appraisees.

Halo effect **:** The appraiser/rater commits an error in evaluating the performance of the appraisee on the basis of a single trait like—appearance, punctuality, co-operativeness etc. A certain positive trait of a person may ignore all other characteristics that have to be considered while evaluating performance.

Leniency effect : The situation where the appraiser gives high ratings and only positive feedback to the appraisee, irrespective of his actual performance. The main reason for leniency may be the appraiser's desire to maintain a cordial relationship with the appraisee.

Stringency effect : An appraiser who feels that the rules and standards of the organisation are not strict enough, tries to be strict in rating his appraisees.

Regency effect : An employee, who has performed well for the preceding nine months but failed to maintain the same level of performance in the last three months preceding the appraisal, may get the same rating as, someone who performed well only in the last 2-3 months of the appraisal period. This is due to the regency effect.

Primacy effect : The performance of the appraisee at the beginning of the appraisal period dominates the evaluation.

Central tendency effect : It is the tendency of the appraiser to rate most of the appraisee in the middle of the performance.

Perceptual set : When a perceived low performer exceeds the expectations of his appraiser, his performance is judged higher than it deserves to be may distort the perception and judgment of actual performance.

USES OF PERFORMANCE APPRAISAL

Apart from evaluating the performance of the employees for rewards/punishments a good performance appraisal system has many other uses. Some of these are listed below-

- Training and development needs of the employees can be determined.
- The performance appraisal system forms the basis for compensation management transfers, promotions and other career planning activities.

- It helps in improving organisation effectiveness and thereby improving the individual performances of the employees.
- It helps in succession planning in the organisation to evaluate human resources of the firm based on the competency, skill set and potential of the workforce.
- It helps in evaluating and auditing the existing plans, processes and systems in the organisation.
- It helps in cross-functional transfers and job enrichment exercises etc., based on inputs from the appraisal system.

MODEL QUESTIONS

1. Explain performance appraisal with its objectives.
2. Explain different methods of appraisals.
3. Write short notes on Behaviourally anchored rating scale(BARS), 360 degree performance appraisal, team appraisals and balanced scorecard method.
4. Explain the drawbacks in performance appraisal system.
5. Focus on appraisal interview.

Chapter

11 The Organisational Implications of Successful Technological Change

CONCEPT

Every organisation has a goal and the organisation structure is one of the forces that affects the goal of the organisation. It designed in such a manner as to serve as an instrument to accomplish the social goal. The efficiency and the extent to which an organisation is able to achieve its goal, are, to a great extent, determined by its structure. So, a structure is developed to give the shape to as tentative idea though about at the initial stage. The structure in beginning is very simple because the size of organisation is small. It becomes complex and needs planning and a systematic approach as the organisation expands. At this stage a well planned and designed structure emerges out.

In a large industrial unit, where services of a large number of people are required, there is always a problem of assigning duties and delegating authority in order to achieve the organisation objective. The organisation structure is influenced by technology as it is being affected by the environment. Different technologies influence the differences in operational procedures. Also, let us see the impact of technology on different elements of organisation like:

ORGANISATION STRUCTURE AND DESIGN

Organisation structure is the pattern in which various parts or components are interrelated so it establishes the relationship among various position and activities in the organisation.

Organisation structure is the differentiation of functions to facilitate the achievement of goals. Jobs are differentiated according to the nature and specialization of jobs. Technological changes are differentiation for the improvement of the process. People are motivated to perform their jobs effectively.

Design of Organization

Any organisation consisting of its members is to function and adhere for achieved goals in forms of goods and services. The behaviour of members is accounted for their assigned duties. Because, duties of persons and identified for causes and effects of the organisation.

The design of any organisation is accounted for creation of uniqueness of rules and turbulent environment that create a model emphasising a relation between persons and management of the organisation. Better design makes behaviour sound and effective. The suitability of the design depends on the nature of work and environment. In behavioural science three designs are accepted like : The first one is simple structure where span of control has only two or three vertical levels and loose employee command. Then next is bureaucratic structure which has narrow span of control, scalar chain of command, functional departmentalisation, centralised authority and highly formalised functions. The activities are divided into highly specialised structures to make the functions effective. And the last one is matrix structure which is a combination of departmentalisation, functionalisation and product. Here, employees have to carry various responsibilities according to the nature of work, hierarchy and position.

Skill and Labour Demands

It has been practically observed that those organisations which have contributed more in changing their skill base have prospered most. Because, the individual was offered the opportunity of constant skill development. The idea was to provide better opportunities for skill development. Thus, a long-term work force created which may be used for learning.

When a new technology is adopted it is accompanied by a number of features like in case of traditional jobs there is need for employees to work in teams. The traditional jobs and groups are those where tasks are largely well defined and controlled. There are little changes. In the modern developed jobs computer control systems has become more and more sophisticated and useful to reduce the technical uncertainty. Now the requirements are increasing and changing and require that the organisations should be more flexible and responsive to the needs and demands. The traditional companies are introducing new technology and new manpower in the labour market. They may be useful hence retraining is needed.

The population growth requires that the companies have to fulfill the requirement of new products and processes and not to retaining or recruitment. The trend shows that skill will reduce and the organisation will have to provide more interesting and stimulating jobs.

Employment Patterns

The technological changes attract the employment pattern for the technologist and those affected by the impact of technology.

The technologists are those who have the understanding of the technology and the skill of its use. But sometimes they feel neglected within the organisation. Therefore, the dashing and frustrated people often start their own organisation.

In an organisation every section have separate planning and objective. Technology is transferred from one section to the other which is not effective because it is a challenge to manage the change process.

The impact of technological change can be wide and different as it has it's impact on the market forces, new capital investment as well as manpower. At some places the demand and supply ratio has to be efficient and qualitative for the effective running of the organisation. Suggestion schemes can be effective and can generate new ideas and introduce change. Some of the guidelines are:

- Quick action to be taken on good ideas.
- Follow them up with individual and his team.
- The head of the team is to be involved.
- Others are to be encouraged to initiate their new and good ideas.
- Managerial resources are to be provided to any programme.

Quality Circle

The multifunctional teams manage change. Quality circles are part of managing change these days. The success of this depends upon the will and desire to improve quality.

The important issues are the scope of such teams activity, the support they receive and their scope for implementation. Innovative companies have evolved the concept of quality circles dealing with immediate problems towards creativity teams. To make the idea effective its working must be demonstrated and practiced from top to bottom.

Attraction and Selection

The selection of the right person is very difficult. It is difficult to decide as to who is innovative and ready to face the innovative culture. In course of face interview there are chances of selection of different types and aptitudes of people. This has been proved by a number of research studies.

There are some guidelines about the proper selection, training and its success. Innovation is uncertain and risky process it has high potential rewards. Therefore, to promote innovation innovative environment is required, where people with different potentialities can get the opportunity to be innovative. In this way individuals will select themselves their choice of job through achievement.

There are some initiatives which can promote innovation and change.

- Top management should be interested for the improvement in ideas at all levels of the organisation.
- The job of the managers can be secured only when they are innovative and make change in the old system.
- Making creativity and innovation a key performance measure through appraisal and performance management systems.
- The scheme of reward, promotion and developing those people who promote change.

Pay System

Sometimes, it is found that the pay objectives do not match with the business objectives. The pay system should match the future prospect of the company. The pay system should be on the basis of individual contribution. An innovative and successful individual deserves for it but sometimes it is difficult to measure an individual's contribution. Because, it is a team work which may lead to success over a long period of time. Short term measures based on individual activity discourage innovations. So, the short tern measures are not helpful for the company.

Employee Involvement

The employee involvement can be more useful if it considers market demand for bringing about the required change and opportunity accordingly. Then the focus of the objective can shift from only problem solving to creative teams to make opportunities for the future. Sometimes, people stick to their jobs and do not interfere in other people's work and activity.

At times, the only thing unchallengeable is the purpose of the business itself.

This openness and challenge is a stroke to management on their position of power and control to influence their organisation. In this situation employee involvement becomes both real and difficult.

As employee involvement can affect some people in position and their status is likely to be affected such quarters may oppose such initiative. Sometimes, the challenge arises when employee involvement is invited through mechanisms like quality circles, problem solving groups and suggestion schemes.

Suggestion Schemes

Suggestion scheme is one of the low priority areas of the companies. Most companies put on the wall a letter box, written on it-suggestion. But the process has become ineffective and neglected, due to a number of factors.

There are a number of guidelines to make suggestion scheme effective like :

- Give quick feed back;
- Take ideas seriously;
- Follow them up with the individual and with their team;
- Involve the work team's boss;
- Praise the imitative, whatever be the quality of the idea;
- Demonstrate quick action on good ideas.

People System

People system obstruct innovation within organisations. For example, the pay system, the way the organisation communicates and how it recruits etc. The personnel profession develops on the basis of a set of system and procedures, which bring consistency, order and conformity to an organisation.

IMPACT OF TECHNOLOGY ON TRADE UNION

The first post-war trade union interest was seen during the early 1960. The impact of which was automation on working people and their trade unions. There were apprehensions that because of more mechanisation, jobs would be cut in the manufacturing sector. But no such crisis was observed. Again with the introduction of electronics during late 1970s and early 1980s the trade union felt that it would be major cause of job reduction. This fear and economic stagnation gave a pressure to maintain jobs and emphasis was placed upon 'new technology agreements'. These were considered to be a means by which the introduction of technological change would be negotiated or jointly decide upon between trade unions and management. These agreements provided communications and consultative structure which helped in bringing the desired change.

The new technology proved ineffective because of several reason. It should be concerned either with trade unions or management in solving the problems of job reduction, job security, pay, retraining and flexibility.

Without any job security the people can not be helpful for giving suggestions for improvement.

Moreover the power of the trade union varies and depends on a number of factors. There may be the interests of the employees related with the introduction of the advanced level technology and so on.

The challenging question for the managers are:

- Who is responsible for managing the organisational implications for technological change in your organisation?
- Up to what extent these are relevant and useful for your organisation.
- How much your technologists are aware of these implications?
- Does your corporate strategy recognise the impact it has on technological innovation and investment?

In getting conclusion of given study, there is found the most crucial challenge to industrial/business organisations to motivate human behaviour towards higher productivity and greater work efficiency. These two factors are most important in respect of satisfying organisational climate for achieving goals in different types.

The organisational climate refers to external and internal environmental conditions in which the organisation exists and grows for achievements of goals to the people. The external factors indicate various factors such as (*a*) cultural/social system, (*b*) science and technology systems.

Though, in India the upsurge in industrial activity requires a through evaluation of our approach for better considerations of technologies. For intense, in agricultural sectors, there would be better optimisation of input resources like seed soil conditioning, fertiliser-micronutrient mixes, pesticides and so on necessitating changes in overall agricultural management. The management provides the potential areas of employment laid on value added agro-food industry. Also the potentiality is credited in fields of cereals, milk, fruits, vegetables and horticulture, floriculture, mushroom cultivation, etc., which create extended form of employment opportunities. The opportunity is laid in absorption of large number of persons in the field of agro-food industries/business around the sector.

In the industrial and manufacturing sector the use of modern electronic and hi-tech gadgets are continual features in term of resurgence of engineering industries, machine tools, foundry, electrical machinery and transport equipment alienated with industrial/business organisations. Moreover, India is an important world in leading software for manufacturing to acquire rapid re-orientation in the coming millennium for inducing new technologies that are introduced in the economy. The rapid industrialisation absorbs only a fraction of unemployed youth.

Thus, the increasing interconnectivity across sectors like structure and manufacturing has spurred the demand for services directly related to such sectors—usually known as focus area for development Hence, with substantial truth, India emerges as a global leader in the services sector with its vast and skilled human resources being its core strength. The services are accounted for trade, storage, transport and communication and finance where all they are counted for the following:

1. total review of the skill;
2. development system for better match between demand and supply; the organisational implications of successful;
3. identification of thrust area; and
4. creation of new demands in sectors like manufacture—telecom, power, roads, posts, media or infotech by means of technological changes in the organisation.

Thus, technological changes have brought scenario of sustained growth of GDP, economic and social infrastructure for building competence in the sector for implementation of maximum benefits.

In these regards, an explanation may be given for vision of the new millennium comprising of social and economic empowerment of human being that would lead economic prosperity in realisation of new vision. The vision justifies organisational climate showing influences on job involvement which is a necessary condition. The condition stresses on level of aspirations and the degree of internationalisation of the organisation affecting the job involvement of the employee in different sectors such as managerial policy and its practice, personal policy and its practice, standard performance, and competency showing the result of recognition and reward etc. Further, the technological changes identify the highest impact on the measures of organisational performance and stepwise forward regression is performed there.

In addition to, the impact of technological changes on the organisations is understood for its culture comprising of (*a*) a pattern of basic assumptions, (*b*) indentation, discovery and development followed by a given group, (*c*) learning in order to cope with its problem of external adaptation and internal integration, (*d*) working conditions in valid forms, and (*e*) correct way to perceive, think and feel in relation to complex problem for the new entrants to the organisation with strong belief, considerable effort and definite desire. Because, the effectiveness of the organisation has been defined as the ability of organisation to mobilise its center of power for action, production and adaptation following positive responses for achieving orientation in forming participative culture.

Thus, the technological changes bring greater impact on the organisation with adoption of elements of review, reflect redirect, reorient, renew human resources in it through a continuous process of individual and collective developmental initiatives for a closed step to organisation effectiveness linked with instruments, processes and outcomes in dealing with job challenge, freedom of action, delegation, responsibility and planning in standard forms.

MODEL QUESTIONS

1. How much the technologists are associated to these implications?
2. Explain about those responsible for managing the organisational implications of technological changes.
3. Whether our corporate strategy identifies the impact it has on technological innovation as well as investment.

Chapter

12 Role of Technology in Human Behaviour

CONCEPT

Organisational behaviour is heavily influenced by undergoing technological changes. These changes can make behaviour useful and beneficial for an organisation. Hence it is necessary for an organisation to be successful, to keep a close watch on this aspect and attain smooth change of technology.

Internet technology: All organisations have immensely improved their efficiency and productivity through information technology as computer culture has revolutionized organisational working. The technology has touched and improved all processes—marketing, production, human development and conduct, financial analysis as well as control. Since the technology is also quite easy and convenient to handle, no organisation can now be imagined to be working without it. The technology also helps in proper decision making process and the same is now based on scientific basis and analysis. Time and money saving have been unprecedented due to adoption of this technology.

Robots: While soft and routine jobs are handled through normal functioning, hard and dangerous functions have also reached within the scope of easy solutions through technologies like robotics, etc. A combination of mechanical and computer engineering, the device has humanised difficult mechanical performance.

Inter dependence of groups and departments: It is evident that modern technology while revolutionising quality and speed, also leads to interdependence. As different groups are getting more and more dependent on it, it is necessary for different personnel to have coordination and avoid working in isolation.

Need for upgraded skills: Special mention has to be made of quality improvement as machine performs the job much more efficiently than a man can. This has necessitated upgradation of skills and workers now need to have higher level of education and understanding. Unlike the previous times, no organisation can now afford to have illiterate or semi-literate workers as working on the highly sophisticated machines requires a minimum level of education, intelligence, and skill.

For an organisational structure, technology has become as vital and significant as environment. Organisations using high technology produce large batches of goods. Processes involving intermittent production adopt sophisticated technology. In such cases span of control and competence are very high.

Creation of a scientific environment: For any organisation, it is important to have a healthy technological philosophy. Organisation's social system has to be scientific with maximum workers having scientific bent of mind. It is a team work and a joint effort of the social sub-system and technical sub-system. Influence of technology on the working of the system is as much as of the environment.

Fear of retrenchment: Like management and personnel, new technology has wielded big impact on labour too. While educated workers have welcomed new technology in the interest of higher production and efficiency, there has always worked a fear of retrenchment and unemployment in the mind of the workers. Since machine increases production and efficiency, workers always fear that the machine may rob them of their job. Here the role of management is to alleviate the feeling that may be prejudicial to adoption of new technology in industrial houses sparking avoidable clashes and loss of morale.

Technological coordination: For a smooth and fruitful changeover, technological approach is always helpful. A technological attitude makes the working extremely smooth, easy and productive. While specialisation leads to creation of different segments in an organisation, it is necessary that different departments work in close coordination and have as frequent exchange of views as possible. This will be possible only if people though working in different departments, are technology savvy and have basic understanding to appreciate others' requirement and coordinate their working. This becomes all the more necessary as all technologies are interrelated and dependent on each other. Environment in an organisation also undergoes change with the change in technology.

Behaviour change: It is obvious that there is all round improvement in workers' skill where new technology is adopted. It improves their professionalism, productivity, and performance. Since working on the new system gives better and cleaner results, and also minimises physical risks compared to the old system, there flows general acceptance to the new technology in the organisations. That changes employees' behaviour and they become more responsible to the organisation and the society with new team spirit, motivation, and goal.

Resistance to change: Since technology is ever progressing and changing, it is necessary for an organisation to constantly upgrade and change its working machinery in the interest of efficiency, productivity and quality improvement. Individual organisations and managers who appreciate this aspect are successful and lead in today's competitive environment. However, though change is constant and inevitable, human psyche is always opposed to change and seeks status quo. This resistance can be both at the level of workers as well as of the organisation.

At individual level, the opposition can be due to selective perception, lack of communication or fear of retrenchment due to apprehension about individual capability to adopt the change. For an organisation to oppose frequent changes may be due to reluctance to invest and also lack of adequate appreciation of the usefulness of the change.

Team vision : It is therefore, necessary that the changing process be analysed systematically before being given a final shape. There should be a comprehensive and detailed exchange of views and thinking that look at the pattern as a whole rather than focussing on individual departments. Further surfacing and testing models are important to make people aware of their existence and modification if required. The employees in an organisation have to have a shared vision thereby facilitating smooth operation of changing process. Team and community vision ensures a dedicated involvement and commitment necessary for any organisation. During the process of change, best results are achieved if there is team learning in the handling of problems and results.

PROCESS OF TECHNOLOGICAL CHANGES

Process of technological innovation is regarded change that involves moving from the present stage towards an innovated desired state promising efficiency, profit and quality improvement. Growth depends on how well and fast an organisation responds favourably to the required new technology necessary for further development. As the new innovation relates to economic growth, global competition, far reaching social and demographic changes, organisations that do not opt to change are left behind in the race of progress and development. Even a top level organisation can come down to nadir if it does not have a mechanism sensitive to technological changes and consequent socio-economic repercussions of the same.

Innovation defined : Innovation is a novel way of doing a work that leads to radical changes in our thinking, motivation, and production. In economic terms innovation leads to positive growth in value as well as improved quality of products ultimately resulting in greater reputation and industrial output. Its goal is positive change for better state of things and standards besides improved productivity. The factors linked to innovation are therefore critical for policy makers of any organisation as decision making is one of the most fateful step in this process. It is a matter involving the future of an organisation linked to performance and the organisation's business standing, competitive positioning, and prestige.

Change steps : The change process involves developing, applying, launching, and managing the implementation of the creative ideas for fruition.

Development : Innovation development means evaluation, modification and suggesting improvements in the present state of affairs. Innovation can be modest or drastic as per the state of affairs. The creative idea throws up a plan for action promising improvement both in quality as well as quantity. It may also include an idea suggesting improved sales or international standing of the product.

Application : The next stage is application where an organisation uses the innovated suggestion and studies how it can be applied and points out the scope of application. The new idea may apply to design, manufacturing, or delivery of new products and services. Here the idea is implemented into action and is transformed into goods or services. The goods now produced are expected to improve substantially and the innovated formula application may also improve the over all quality of various other products of the company. An example is the innovation in radar technology whose application led to over all improvement in general electrical components which now became more slick and small. A new technology can be further improved and its application to more products and goods is an ongoing matter of study and research.

Launching : Next comes the step when the new application is adopted and launched as programme and product of the company. Here the organisation introduces new products and services in market. This stage is vital as the fate of the new innovation, its success or failure depends on its acceptability and popularity among the customers and in business circles. While the idea is no doubt creative, it is a matter of great significance involving even a chance element if the end users would feel enthusiastic about it. Hence success and failure of an idea, irrespective of its novelty and brilliance, depends on many external factors often not under control of their creator.

Application growth : Post launch the stage comes for application growth. This is the time for high economic performance. In case of demand generation, an organisation has to meet the supply adequately. Since there is usually not a very close analysis of the demand generation at the product launching stage, supply of goods initially low, mostly remains short of the demand. Here, though difficult, correct forecasting of demand plays an important role and organisations who do this prosper in the competitive growth. At the same time undue optimism about the demand can also lead to glut of the product in market and unsold goods may sit in warehouses for years. This state may cause loss in business and diversion of funds to non-demand and unproductive areas.

Innovative maturity : After a stage of growing demand there comes a period of innovative maturity as various other companies come into the market using the innovated technology, some with improved features and reduced costs. Such pretenders though promising better service and quality are not benefited substantially because as secondary producers they arrive at the stage late by the time the original company is already established. Still they do manage to wean away some of the customers who are fence sitters and are not much conscious about the market forces and philosophies. This arrival time of this stage of maturity depends on the simplicity or complexity of the originally innovated idea—how easy it is to copy. Normally a business idea if it can be copied easily, spreads as a universal practice fast. However, if the formula is complicated and involves some original or unique application, it can remain unassailed for a longer time. Moreover, if the skills needed to implement it are rare and difficult to imitate, the pretenders may feel foxed for long and remain in dark and the product enjoys a longer stay at the top without facing any imitation or competition.

Decline : Every new innovation has a time period till it remains new and in demand. It has to become old sooner or later and by the time it reaches the maturity stage, the profits have reached their optimum growth. Now comes the stage of innovation decline when the innovation has to be substituted with new ideas and inventions. With the market being glutted with various duplicate and competitive products, the original innovative profits face depletion and slowly become stagnant. All organisations therefore, must nurture an atmosphere where their innovators, engineers and creative workers are continuously encouraged not to sit back but constantly innovate. Research and development department these days finding a place in most organisations, should be flush with funds and facilities where the personnel working there are always busy in thinking, deliberating, experimenting and coming out with new innovations. Success has a pyramid structure and it is just not possible to continue to remain at the top indefinitely. A thoughtful management keeps encouraging its scientists and workers to constantly explore and come out with new suggestions about improvements in system as well as in products. Organizations that are conscious of this aspect process all suggestions seriously whether they are from employees or from the public.

Social problems : While organisations keep encouraging their research and development workers to keep innovating, personnel officers have also to remain ever sensitive to various human and social problems falling out of the technological changes. Changes endanger social problems much faster than the society finds solution to them. Lest such problems retard the growth of an organisation, the concerned officials have to remain pro-active and study as well as implement reforms in their working systems so that the impact of such fall out is minimised. This calls for new types of supervision, new reward system and a totally new thinking in organisational matters and employees relationship.

Red tape : As reforms are need at a faster pace, maladies like red tape have to be eliminated as they delay the process of change and may even defeat it. A fresh look at procedures and systems operations should be undertaken to analyse if procedures though old and honoured, have now become redundant and creating impediments in the path of growth and implementation. Periodic meetings and inter-departmental consultations if done frequently can help minimise this situation and lead to newer methods that help in growth and higher productivity. No individual or egoistic aspects should stand in the way of improved and better functioning and streamlining of a system.

Resistance to change : Management should also take a view at the factors responsible for resistance to change. Beside procedural obstacles, the resistance may be due to lack of education and self confidence among the workers. Since the technology is new, workers may feel less confident handling it and may fear relegation or even termination of their jobs. Here comes the role of the management to ensure the employees about their future growth and prospects. Besides, training programmes for absorbing the new style of working and technology and more and more refresher courses should regularly take place to avoid this sort of time and efficiency lag. Industrial engineers and personnel officers may be given training in human relations. In order to overcome the human effects of poorly designed system, they should be trained to handle psychological problems pumping frustration quite often prevalent among the less educated and semi or non-skilled workers. That will maintain a healthy team spirit and cordial working environment imperative for the growth of an organisation and conducive to new innovations and research.

Fear of identity loss : Another human problem arising out of the technological innovations is the fear of individual identity loss. Technology has created millions of new types of jobs and systems with human relevance taking a back seat. This loss of social significance where machine and technology are paramount, a worker feels himself lost, unrecognised, and some times even redundant or insignificant. This loss of social status is likely to pump in frustration and hinder initiative on the part of employees. Management has to check this feeling of alienation and work on a new environment wherein employees may feel themselves more relevant and useful. Technology has no doubt made working more simplified. It should however, not imply that employees' involvement is not needed.

Conclusion

In the modern age of global competition and business, no organisation can work in isolation and remain immune to changes. Scientific and technological innovations proceeding at a fast pace all round have made the world an arena of new skills where only the fittest will survive and those who cannot adapt to changes will face extinction and perish. It is obligatory for organisations to change their systems and working timely lest they are left behind in the race for progress. At the same time, modern business cannot ignore the humanitarian aspect of the situation or neglect its employees who are the backbone of any organisation. It is therefore the biggest challenge before the present day's management to bring about the change as softly and amicably as possible. With new methods yielding place to new, management has to impress upon the employees to learn new skills and adopt changes so that they remain relevant to the new ways of working. Those who have skill and initiative should be encouraged to change their profession and working and be absorbed with dignity in the new set up. Focus should be on absorption to the maximum extent so that the change is painless and heralds a new era of progress and prosperity not only for the management but for all.

MODEL QUESTIONS

1. Discuss technological innovations.
2. Write notes on Internet technology and robotics.
3. Discuss social problems with respect to technological change.
4. Explain Red tape and innovative maturity.
5. Explain steps of technological innovations.

Chapter

13 Organisational Technologies

Introduction

One central and most significant element for effective operation in management is technology without which it is these days almost impossible to perform. No organisation can afford to ignore the fast developing changes in almost all the fields of management and have strong impact on institutional working, progress, productivity and profiteering. A unit may be large or small, produce modestly or in a big way. Irrespective of the size, an organisation has to be aware that constant upgradation of its production tools, methods and working is as essential as any other component attached high priority so far. Each technology is associated with a particular organisation structure and has to be nurtured, nourished, and improved as a continuous process.

Benefits of New Technology

Every new innovation is a landmark in the functioning of an organisation. While it saves money by reducing the number of working hands, it boosts profits through increased production and improved quality of goods produced. New technology also reduces costs by minimising waste, optimum utilization of material, and reducing production error to a negligible extent.

A look at some examples where new technology has been introduced can substantiate our contention that during the last three decades, working in all organisations has undergone revolutionary changes resulting into all round positive developments in almost every field of management and business. For example, information technology has done wonders and changed the face of working of all the departments in every field. The technology has made unprecedented inroads into all the fields boosting organisational potency through improved performance, fastest possible communication, and faultless operations.

Automated System

True globalisation has come via its automated system that has demolished all barriers of distances, seas, and other man made impediments. The system competes well with an Alladin's genie being not only efficient but also cheap and as swift as lightning. A new era common language of communication has dawned where communication is instant, flawless, and direct no more dependant on any messengers subject to their individual capacity, whims and callousness. To take the cake, all this electrifying achievement has been attained at a ridiculously low cost.

IT and the World

Thanks to IT, face of the world today stands totally changed with people from far off continents across the oceans chatting and communicating with each other undisturbed and in a secure relaxed state as if conversing to their next door neighbour. The technology has also blasted the concept of high rise and exhorbitantly costly palacial offices which like the feudal lords are facing gradual extinction. Time is not far when prototypes of some of the world famous offices will be placed in museums where the onlookers will be reminded of the grand past like the days of mighty empires whose lofty accounts can be found in the pages of the history. Constructing huge buildings to start a new business now is becoming redundant as almost all vital and important operations can be performed from the comforts and friendly atmosphere of individual homes and apartments. This has drastically reduced the operation costs and its impact is now visible in all fields including transport, commutation, electricity bills, maintenance, etc.

IT has penetrated almost every aspect of our daily lives engulfing business, leisure, and the entire society. Personal computer, fax machines, mobile phones, pagers, and Internet are the universal and common language of communication that has made the universe more cosmopolitan and friendly. Breaking all barriers of class and privileges, mobile phones can today be seen as a technology in use by even the lowest class of workmen and people. These new instruments have heralded an era of increased productivity, greater profitability, and clutter free working conditions for all irrespective of any distinctions like developed or developing, high or low, rich or poor. Transactions can be made worldwide over phones or through e-mails sitting in one's office or even home.

Through automation we can design our work totally on machines. Automated operations work speedily with little error. The system also improves product quality and boosts production. Being not subject to human error, margin of fault is also negligible.

Computed Manufacturing

Extensions of automation revolve around computer-assisted manufacturing. Here it is the job of computers to design and manufacture products and the whole operation is smooth. Computer can quickly produce a desired product, prepare labels and copies of orders, and disseminate the product to its destination. Closely aligned with this system is computer-integrated manufacturing which takes the production to a more complex level and results are automated and faultless.

Robotics

While programming and soft business can be discharged with least disturbance, even the heavy manual functions like movement of bulky goods and products can be discharged through computer operated robotic work units. Robotics is the technology where construction, maintenance and delivery can be given effect through machines instead of man. Robotic operations have been increasingly in use sine 1980. Needless to say, this system does away with huge labour costs involved in operation of goods from one place to the other that is subject to human whims and caprices besides the vagaries of weather. Not only costs, the operation being fast lead to a fresh delivery undamaged or undisturbed if executed through human operations. Robotic use is more in welding, loading and unloading of goods, painting and finishing, and casting. In machine operations like cutting, grinding, polishing, drilling, sanding, and buffing, use of robotic technology is on increase. Inspection work is also being increasingly taken over by robots gradually. Not long ago companies like Dailmer Chrysler had replaced 200 welders with 50 robots thereby reducing operation cost by 20 per cent besides bringing about a neat accident free safe operation system. Trend is now for all manufacturers big or small to apply the robots in their working which ultimately turns out to be much cheaper, safer, and hassle free drastically eliminating the hazards involved in damages and litigation due to hurt or accidents caused during manual operations.

Boost in Service Technology

Automation has also boosted service technology worldwide. In banking sector for example, automated teller machines have made the operations fast, accurate, and easy irrespective of remote locations. Offices are now sending employees' salary cheques directly to banks thus eliminating a lot of accounts work and long queues of employees waiting to receive their wages every month. Banks have also fixed teller machines at places where the account holders can draw their amount easily and need not go to banks cashiers for the same. The whole procedure has now become simpler, quick, convenient, fast, and hassle free. Elimination of manual operations has led to speedy and better disposal of work multi fold every where.

Video and Mobile Phones

Another device of automation—video and mobile phones, can now be seen every where in use. Video-on-demand is in effective use and can even supplement in-service training sessions in an organisation. The device can drastically reduce the costs involved in guest lectures involving fees and travel costs, accounting, etc.

Most popular technology is mobile phones. The device is under use by almost every class of society and is convenient as people can be contacted all the time irrespective of location. Landline phones are virtually fast becoming a legend of the past yielding place to ultra-slim beautifully designed sophisticated handy tools equipped with the latest technology and devices. Mobile manufacturers like Nokia, Motorola, Erricson, Idea, Reliance, and many more are in fierce competitive race with their research and development personnel putting their heads together devising new and unique features that will help them remaining one upon the other.

No Alternative to Change

In a competitive global environment, where quality and productivity coupled with cost control are key to success, no organisation can afford to rest on its laurels as old skills are either not relevant or have become completely outdated. Fast changing business techniques and global requirements have made it imperative for organisations to absorb new technology and create a healthy progressive environment through out where people are not averse to learning new things, methods and practices. While white collared staff mostly sees new technology as its enemy and fears retrenchment, management should dispel such fears by organising technical classes and training courses for its workers and absorbing those who are capable to change. A careful planning where workers can be trained for the new environment and skills has to be made and executed in the interest of maintaining industrial peace and harmony. New technology should be planned to fan out people's range of skills and widening their sphere of responsibilities. For those who cannot be accommodated, a golden hand shake policy has to be carved but that should be only the last resort.

Human Approach to Change

Human implications of new technology have to be thought and planned at the design stage itself. Emphasis should be on improving the work environment and exploration of ways to accommodate more and more people into the fold. A socio-technical approach will work positively all round creating a sense of loyalty and dedication among workers and the organisation retaining a trusted useful hand. Workers who thus acquire extra skills will also feel confident and assured about their future. Needless to say, a comprehensive thought has to be given to training and in-service training programmes for the employees aiming at familiarisation with new development through guest lectures and field visits, etc.

Conclusion

It is also in the interest of an organisation to keep and follow an open communication policy about the forthcoming technological changes in the system. All likely to be affected or otherwise concerned must be kept informed and should be kept in picture right from the initial stage. Employees should have access to all information about the changes an organisation intends to bring and the skills that will be required for that. This will forewarn the workers and they will know where they are likely to stand in the new set up. This though delicate, will give them ample time and opportunity to plan their future and how they should change themselves in order to remain relevant to the organisation. Those who can get themselves updated with the addition of some more skills should be encouraged to do so. Since it is a humanitarian aspect, people have a right to know in what manner they are likely to be affected and how they have to meet the new challenges. Management approach has to be to absorb the surpluses as far as possible by absorbing the skilled, natural wastage or voluntary redundancies.

MODEL QUESTIONS

1. Explain the benefits of technologies for the organisations.

Bibliography

A Books

Alexender, K.C., *Participative Management—The Indian Experience.* Shri Ram Centre for Industrial Relations, New Delhi, 1973.

Allen, T.J. *Managing the Flow of Technology,* Cambridge, Mass MIT Press, 1977.

Armstrong, Michales, *Handbook of Personnel Management,* Kigam Page Lte.; London, 1976.

Basu, K.S.; *New Dimensions in Personnel Management,* Mcmillan, New Delhi, 1979.

Beach, Dales; *Personne,* Mcmillan Publishing Co. New York, 1985.

British Institute of Management, *Job Evaluation—A Practical Guide,* London.

Burans, T & G.M. Stalkar, *The Management of Innovation*< London, Tavistock Publications, 1961.

Byars Loyd R. and L.W. Rue, *Human Resource and Personnel Management,* Richard De. Irwin, Illinois, 1984.

Chatterjee, N.N.; *Management of Personnel in Indian Enterprises,* Allied Book Agency New Delhi, 1978.

Devis, Keith, *Human Behaviour at Work,* Tata McGraw Hill, New Delhi, 1985.

Durbin, A.J. *Personnel and Human Resource Management,* D. Van Norhland Co; New York, 1981.

Dwivedi, R.S; *Management of Human Resources,* Oxford and IBH, New Delhi, 1980.

Flippo, Edwin B. *Personnel Management,* McGraw Hill, Kogakusha, Tokyo,1990.

Ghosh, S; *Trade Unionism in Underdeveloped Countries,* Bookland, Calcutta, 1966.

Gupta, C.B; *Managerial and Executive Remuneration in India,* Allied Publishers, New Delhi, 1984.

Halloran, Jack, *Personnel and Human Resource Management, Readings in Personnel Management,* Orient Longman, New Delhi, 1970.

International Labour Organisation, *Labour Management Relations (Report No. 23)* Geneva, 1960.

Kapoor, T.N. (ed), *Personnel Management and Industrial Relations in India,* N.M. Tripathi and Sons Bombay, 1968.

Kudchedkar, I.S. *Aspects of Personnel Management and Industrial* Relations, McGraw Hill, New York, 1979.

Luck, T.J.; *Personnel Administration and Appraisal;* McGraw Hill, 1955.

Mathis, Robert L, and J.H. Jackson, *Personnel Human Resource Management,* West Publishing Co. New York, 1982.

Miner. John B. and M.G. Miner, *Personnel and Industrial Relations.* Mcmillan Publishing Co. New York, 1977.

Monappa, Aruna, *Human Resource Planning and Career Planing,* 11 M Ahmedabed (Mimeo).

Prasad, *Personnel,* Bombay, 1973.

Singh, N.K., *Dimensions of Personnel Management,* Vikas Publishing House, New Delhi, 1984.

Singh, N.K. and G.K Suri (eds). *Personnel Management,* Vikas Publishing House, New Delhi, 1985.

Srivasatava, Suresh (ed.), *Behavioural Sceinces in Management,* Asia Publishing House, Bombay, 1967.

Yoder, Dale and H.G. Henerman, *Handbook of Personnel and Industrial Relations,* Bureau of National Affairs, Washington, 1979.

B. Journals

HRD Newsletter, XLRI Jameshedpur.

Indian Journal of Psychology, New Delhi.

Indian Journal of Social Work, Tata Institute of Social Sciences, Bombay.

Indian Journal of Training and Development, Indian Society for Training and Development, New Delhi.

Labour Chronicle, Bombay.

Index

F

O

P

Q

R

❑❑❑